The Mission Motivated Life

Insights on how to reach out to the human heart

M. Mubiana

The Mission Motivated Life

Copyright © 2013 M. Mubiana

ISBN-13: 978-0615863481

All rights reserved. Written permission must be secured from the publisher to use or reproduce any part of this book, except in the case of brief quotations embodied in the critical articles and reviews.

DEDICATION

This book is dedicated to those who were instrumental in helping me to learn from the word of God and this includes Reverend Everisto Mateyo who led me to the Lord and answered most of my Bible questions at the beginning of my Christian life. This also includes Reverend Lazarus Chitalu, the pastor who together with the church in Kafue prayed and sent me off into missions. I will not forget Randy and Jane Rhodes my base leaders at Youth With A Mission in Lusaka who opened the door for me into my first experience in missions and Reverend Jamie Eitson in Tyler who welcomed me with open arms in his church as a minister on the mission field. I will always be grateful to the Lord for you all.

CONTENTS

	Acknowledgments	i
Chapter 1	God's Gift to the World	9
Chapter 2	Signs of Faith	15
Chapter 3	Inner Healing	21
Chapter 4	The Love of God	28
Chapter 5	The Will of God	37
Chapter 6	The Gifts to the Church	45
Chapter 7	The Holy Spirit	56
Chapter 8	True Identity	63
Chapter 9	Spiritual Warfare	67
Chapter 10	Confronting Forces of Darkness	74
Chapter 11	Taking Care of Yourself	80
	About the Author	89

ACKNOWLEDGMENTS

I am very grateful to my wife Jane K. Mubiana for all the encouragement she gave me when I was writing this book.

Chapter 1

God's Gift to the World

God has a mission on earth and it aims at reaching the human heart. For us this mission begins when we receive the gift that God has given. No one can buy that gift and no one can give it, but God alone. Any gift from God is special. What makes any gift from God so special? Well, just like all other gifts that have ever been given to anyone, a gift from God is surely accompanied by gracious thoughts toward the receiver. The gift of God says, "I think well of you and I understand your situation therefore I would like to do for you that which no one can do". Thoughts behind God's gifts position the receiver for precious reserves that he has kept for those who respond favorably.

The gift of God cannot be bought by any man. Other gifts in the world have been bought and sold, but any gift from God cannot be bought. In Acts 8:18 the Bible in reference to the gift of the Holy Spirit says, "And when Simon saw that through laying on of the apostles' hands the Holy Ghost was given, he offered them money"(KJV). It was wrong for Simon to offer money because any gift from God cannot be bought. Every gift from above is free for all of us.

The gift that God has given to the world is the gift of his own son Jesus Christ. It is in Jesus Christ where we all find the forgiveness of sins and that makes him a perfect gift for us all since the whole world needs salvation from the bondage of sin. When someone does not receive this gift, such a one has no life. This gift cannot be earned or received by good religious behavior. The one and only way to receive from God is by faith.

Faith is the only way God is pleased. It is also the only way any sinner can be justified. The whole world has missed the mark. We have all sinned against God because Adam and Eve ate of the fruit of knowledge of good and evil. This is the tree God commanded them not to eat from and by eating from it they disobeyed God. That is why through Adam and Eve we have all sinned or missed the mark. Through Adam sin entered the world and now everyone has gone astray. The Bible clearly states that everyone in this world has sinned. This situation breaks God's heart because sin brings death, sickness and suffering.

When people continued to commit sin many years ago, God was grieved. God was grieved because sin brought suffering to his creation. This is the reason why he decided to destroy man with a flood at the time he saved Noah and his family. If God is capable of feeling sad, it means he is also capable of being pleased. One thing that pleases God is faith.

God justifies people when they have faith. This is the reason why we can say that faith does the impossible. God backs up faith in real life. Through faith people of old obtained righteousness and went on to do great things. Faith is the only thing that pleases God and through faith we can receive any gift from him. This is the way God has ordained for all people to be able to receive what he gives. People can be changed or healed when they have faith.

Long time ago Enoch was translated because he had faith. When God came to fellowship with him, he decided to take Enoch with him. Faith did the impossible that day. A mere mortal was translated and taken into heaven. This only happens when God rewards faith and does the impossible. Faith pleases God.

At the river Jordan as Jesus came up from the water after being baptized in water, God by his audible voice said that he was pleased with Jesus. Jesus pleased God the same way we should all please God. He is our example and the only way to accomplish God's mission successfully is by having faith because that is what pleases God.

When we receive the gift of God's Son Jesus Christ into our hearts, we do it by faith and it pleases God. No one can receive Jesus Christ by good behavior. You have to believe God exists and that he is powerful enough to do anything. This is how people become children of God. They receive Jesus into their hearts by faith. Through this encounter people become children of God. This is the way to enter the Kingdom of God and the beginning a father son relationship with God. This is a new birth experience that establishes that same father son relationship with God.

When God created man and placed him in the Garden of Eden, he created him in his image. Where is this image located? This likeness or image is in man's spirit. Man has a body, soul and spirit. The body is a system of different parts that makes it possible for a man to physically function in this world. The soul is made up of the will, intellect and the emotions and these parts provide a sense of inner self. The spirit part of man is what which gets connected with God and it transcends both soul and body. The spirit part of man is what becomes quickened by God during the new birth experience.

When the new birth occurs, the spirit of a man becomes one with the Spirit of God. The Spirit that comes into man then is the spirit of sonship and this happens because faith is involved. The spirit part of man provides a deeper sense of awareness which is above emotional feelings or a stream of thoughts that usually gives that self-made sense of self. The true sense of self goes much deeper and that is what is known as the inner man.

The inner man or spirit man is dead in sin and trespasses until he is regenerated by God's Spirit because of what Christ has done in his work of redemption. The changes that occur to the spirit man affect feelings, thoughts as well as the behavior of a man as a whole person. Therefore the inner man becomes strong and capable of influencing the whole person when he feeds on the Word of God. This is how man's life changes from the inside out.

Although man can be dead in sin and trespasses, through Christ he can still be made alive. The work that Christ has done for us at the cross has made it possible for us to have our inner man made alive. This experience is exemplified in water baptism because those who receive Christ are identified with him in his death and resurrection. This is the reason why water baptism symbolizes the death and resurrection of Christ and as we identify with him in his death we also rise to a new life. It is through this experience that man becomes a partaker of God's divine nature.

Walking in the newness of life is only possible in Christ. Jesus has made this new life possible for us because he died and rose again for our justification. This is the way anyone can become a new creation. As a new creation the old way of life passes away and a new way gets established.

Through this precious gift from God we receive every good and perfect gifts such as eternal life, forgiven of sin and much more. However, to receive this gift of the person of Jesus Christ, you just have to invite him to come into your heart. This is something you do because you believe Jesus Christ died for your sins and that he arose for your justification. His life will manifest as you continue to yield to him. The change of life is really made possible by the Spirit of God and not by religious traditions. Yielding your live to God through Jesus Christ is what makes this possible.

Living by faith helps a believer to be victorious against sin. A believer does not have to work hard at trying to be a good Christian. Believers do not need to work so hard at keeping a Christian appearance. It is not about maintaining a religious poise, but about yielding to Jesus who makes this new life possible. A believer must always pray because his communion with God makes the new life possible. This new life is made possible by God's Spirit. The end of faith in your life is the salvation of your soul and it also deals with any of all your troubled spots in your life. He will always deal with storms of life if you allow him.

One day Jesus was with the disciples on a ship. When they were on their way Jesus fell asleep on a pillow and as he was sleeping a storm arose. The disciples tried everything they could to try to save themselves from possible destruction. In the middle of all this commotion Jesus was peacefully sleeping on a pillow below deck. When they called on him he just spoke to the storm with authority and the storm ceased. The disciples were amazed at what happened and gloried God, but Jesus looked at the disciples and rebuked them for not having enough faith to deal with the storm. Jesus wants us to have faith. Faith takes care of real life situations and this includes natural circumstances that we face day by day.

Having faith is really taking God at his Word. This means taking what God says as having value enough to deal with our real life situation. Jesus teaches us to be of good courage because in this world we will always have trials, but we have to be courageous because he has overcome the world. Our faith in Christ is what makes us overcome the world. What Jesus Christ says is what we depend on in order to overcome. When Jesus told the disciples to go to the other side of the lake, but ended up in a storm, all they needed to know is that every circumstance they faced on the way had no power because of what Jesus said to them. If the disciples got hurt in the storm they could have blamed Jesus. In fact they blamed him for sleeping below deck while they struggled in the storm. They did not need to blame him because what they really needed was faith. What we all need in our circumstances is faith. When God asks you to do something, you should be able to see that obstacles will not stop the fruition of what he has spoken. What Jesus says is dependable.

Without hearing the word of God one cannot have faith. When the disciples got on the ship with Jesus because he told them to get to the other side, they had faith in him. Jesus was responsible for the trip and the disciples trusted that it was going to be alright. When they got into a storm and had run out of options they had to call on Jesus. God is the author of life and consulting him in time of need is the right thing to do. When people face difficult times, they need to consult God and this is what faith is all about. When the disciples called upon Jesus he was asleep. Jesus is not here physically, but his presence is here by his Spirit. We cannot see him physically, but his presence is made available to us by his Spirit. He dwells in us by faith and when you call upon him in faith he hears and responds.

Chapter 2

Signs of Faith

The signs of faith represent manifestations of the workings of God. There is a difference between the work of man and the work of God. The work of man is done within the limits of the laws of nature, but the work of God transcends the laws of nature. The work of God manifests what we call miracles.

Faith ushers people into doing exploits that is why the people who had faith in ancient times performed great wonders. The work of salvation today is the one real thing that God does when we put our faith in him through Jesus Christ. When people come to understand and experience the change of life that comes through faith in Christ they usually tend to wonder why they were not told about it earlier. This signifies that what they have experienced has made a difference and that is why they would like other people to have a similar spiritual experience too.

The realization of this new birth experience as being undeniably a gift of God gives them the passion to try to reach out to other people with the gospel. The message they carry is founded on what God has done for them personally. They know that what God has done for them is what they desire for others.

What God has done for you will entrust you with the mission to reach the human heart. The key to the heart lies in the fact that Christ is doing a life changing work of love in your life. This is not something acquired from Bible College or Seminary. This is all due to the fact that God's love that touches your heart in this life changing experience will also touch other people's hearts.

We have to know that what appeals to the mind is limited to only appeal to another person's mind. Spiritual things that touch your spirit will touch and quicken other people's spirits. This heavenly treasure is poured out from vessel to vessel until the return of Jesus Christ. The true sign of faith then is the change that stems and manifests from that new life experience in Christ. If one does not have this new birth as a life experience, such a one has no message and ultimately no mission.

Ideologies cannot change the message that comes from your own personal experience. In the ninth chapter of the book of John the Bible talks about Jesus healing a man who was born blind. This man is like every one of us born in this world. Remember all have sinned and have come short of the glory of God. This means we are all in spiritual darkness and only Jesus is that light. In verse five of the same chapter the Bible in reference to Jesus says, "As long as I am in the world, I am the light of the world" (KJV).

Since Jesus is the light of the world, he healed this blind man, who from birth experienced life without light. This miracle involved faith because faith is the only thing that pleases God. Jesus exercised faith all the time as he ministered to those in need because faith is the key to the supernatural work of God. Sometimes Jesus asked the recipients if they believed that he could do what they requested of him. When they acknowledged that he was able to do what they desired their miracle ended up manifesting.

At one time when a man who got healed was questioned about how he could now see, he responded according to what he knew well. One thing he knew is that he once was blind, but now he could see. The passing of time could not change the facts of what happened to him. This man's message was then founded in what God had done and what God did could not be refuted or changed. What God does is not like a good idea which can change as time passes. When this man was asked to describe what happened, those who questioned him really aimed at trying to change his view of who Jesus is. They suggested that Jesus was a sinner because he was not keeping the Sabbath since he was healing people on the day of rest he was not really from God.

Those who were accusing Jesus instigated the idea to discredit him. However, no idea or suggestion could change the man who was healed. It was a fact that came out of his experience with Jesus Christ. This man could not be shaken in his faith because the miracle working power of God had impacted his life. When your life has been impacted by the power of God your faith gets rooted in the power of God. Where is your faith today? Is it in human wisdom or in the power of God? If you believe in Jesus Christ then expect manifestations that go beyond natural boundaries. God is a supernatural God and his work is a supernatural work.

Supernatural manifestations are a true sign of faith. When Jesus saw a fig tree and desired to eat from it, but had no figs, he cursed it. He spoke words against that tree and those words caused it to wither in the very same hour. The disciples were surprised that the tree withered in such a short time. Due to this Jesus turned to his disciples and started teaching them about faith and how it causes supernatural manifestations. Faith is also what caused people in ancient days to do the exploits they did. It is still the only way God becomes one with you so as to do his covenant miraculous works.

One day the disciples were sailing on the lake and Jesus approached them walking on water. At first, this frightened them until Jesus identified himself and Peter one of the disciples in the boat asked him if he could get out of the boat to come to him. Jesus called to him saying "come" and Peter got out of the boat and walked on the water to go to Jesus. This was an act of faith and it worked for Peter in the middle of a real life situation. When he was walking toward Jesus he looked at how hard the winds were blowing and began to be fearful. When he got scared and began to sink Jesus helped him from drowning and immediately pointed out to him that he should not have doubted. This event proves that any supernatural walk is only possible where there is faith. Anyone can experience the miraculous walk made possible only by faith.

When you find yourself saying, why was I not told about this Jesus who has made so much of an impression on my life? That is a sign of faith. When you also find yourself filled with passion to tell other people about what Jesus has done for you that is also a sign of faith. All this springs from what God has done in your life because what he has done for you is what he can do for other people too. What has God done for you? What God has done for you is part of what makes the mission motivated life possible.

God wants to turn your life into a powerful message to the world. For you to make sense of what God is doing, your life has to be impacted by the new birth experience. This is what makes it relevant both to you and all those who listen to you. It's not easy to forget a message springing from a real life experience. Such a message makes you a true witness. People must see Jesus and not you. Jesus is that light which enlightens every man in this world. This means through you, God can reach out to other people since he is really within you. In Christ people are able to distinguish light from darkness. Light expels darkness and it cannot be overcome by darkness. Therefore it exposes the human condition of sin and provides guidance.

This is the reason why change in one's life is a good sign of faith. If one claims that he has received Christ in his heart, but does not show visible signs of change in his life, it probably means that such a one has never met Christ. When someone meets Christ, the life of God himself will be present for all to see. The evidence of change in someone's life is a sign that faith has been present. Signs of faith are a manifestation of what is happening in the inner working of things in relation to what the Word of God declares. The manifestation is the proof of what reality is in the spirit world. Faith makes what cannot be seen by the natural eye to be visible. That is why the Bible points out that faith is the substance of things hoped for and the evidence of things not seen.

    The exploits that the people of old did were done by faith. Some of the exploits that were done by young men like Shadrach, Meshach and Abed-nego were done by faith. In the book of Daniel chapter three these young men ended up being thrown into the furnace, but never got consumed by the fire because they had faith that helped them to find deliverance from God. When the fire in the furnace could not have power over them it became proof to the King that their God was the only true God. They had faith in the living God and a great sign occurred to prove the presence of the invisible God.

    There was no guarantee that the three young men were going to be delivered from being consumed by the fire that is why they even told King Nebuchadnezzar that they would still not worship that Idol if God ended up not delivering them. When they were delivered from the fire in the furnace, the king then believed that the God they worshiped was the one and only true God. God rescued the three young men by not allowing fire to consume them. In other words, he approved the young men's actions and delivered them because they had faith in what he says in his word. This was a sign of faith in the one only true God, the maker of heaven and earth. Reaching out to the human heart should be accompanied by the proof that the mission itself is legitimate.

What the Word of God teaches is that faith produces proof. When Jesus cursed the fig tree the tree withered in a short period of time. Jesus still tells us to speak and do things the same way he did. This helps to unveil the truth. The truth reveals the way things really are and that expels falsehood. This is the reason why Jesus had to prove that he is the son of the living God and his resurrection from the dead is the undeniable proof he is truly the son of God. What about you? What proof do you have? Can you prove that now you are a child of God? Can you prove that your life has truly changed because of the new relationship you have with Christ? The way you live will reflect the life in you. Since the nature of God is in you as a child of God you cannot sin. What happens then when you sin? When a child of God gets entangled in sin he or she experiences a great sense of sadness. When you are a child of God it means the nature of God is in you and sin only makes you to feel sad.

Nature is one true dimension of identity that reflects the true characteristics of any living thing. When you are a child of God, you remain a child of God whether someone is watching over you or not. You can move into a city where no one knows you and still uphold the same principles of faith without worrying much about who is watching. You do not need anyone to externally watch your life because you are moved by the Spirit of God within you. Children of God are led by his Spirit from within them and sin has no power over them.

Chapter 3

Inner Healing

People come from different family, cultural, economic or even spiritual backgrounds and their past life experiences impact their present relationships. Life experiences have a bearing on an individual's behavior in any relationship. However, the work that Jesus does in people's lives brings healing. This kind of healing requires recipients to participate in the healing process itself.

In the book of Acts the Bible tells us that Jesus was anointed with the Holy Spirit and Power and that he went about doing good and healing people who were oppressed of the devil. As Jesus went about doing good and healing people, he one day ended up healing a man who was blind. One interesting thing is that both Jesus and the blind man actively participated in the healing process. Jesus stayed with the blind man from the time he met him to the time the healing was completed. This is what happens in inner healing. God's word guides the recipient in the healing process.

The first time Jesus touched his eyes he asked him if he saw anything. The man was honest and answered Jesus correctly by saying that he saw men like trees walking around. Without being honest with Jesus no man can receive inner healing. This tells us that inner healing is a process and the key to this type of healing is the recipient's willingness to participate in the healing process.

The interpretation of what is unfolding in front of you plays a major role in the healing process. Your background can influence the way you look at things, but when you are honest with Jesus during the process nothing can hinder you from receiving from God. How you perceive things will have to line up with the word of God which is the truth. Jesus agreed with the blind man when he said that he saw men looking like trees walking around. This man did not sabotage his miracle by lying about what he saw or experienced.

When you are not honest about how things are, you are not helping in the healing process. If you claim to be healed when you are really not healed, it is a drawback. The appropriate thing to do is to acknowledge him as the miracle worker and to surrender your will to him. This man was willing to let Jesus heal him in any way possible. He was completely surrendered to Jesus because he was honest. If this man had said that he saw everything clearly when in actual fact did not, it could have been a lie. The fact is that a man who was receiving the healing lined up with the truth. Jesus is the truth; we all have to line up with the truth.

When we are bound in sin we are blind, but when we are forgiven we see things clearly. What does the Word of God say? It says that we should forgive those who trespass against us. The fact is that forgiveness has a way of changing our view of those who are considered to be enemies. We have to realize that there are some people who act like enemies, but are actually really friends. Some people pretend to be friends and play the game of friendship for some time when they are really not friends. Your response in both cases matters because your response to each of them can either close or open the door to their hearts. This is one way to really enlarge your heart. An enlarged heart accommodates different types of people. Do you have an enlarged heart? If in doubt, how do you enlarge your heart? Practicing forgiveness is the best way to enlarge your heart because God deals with you the same way you deal with other people who interact with you.

God does not show favoritism. When you forgive, God also forgives you the same way you forgive other people. In Galatians 6:7 the Scripture declares, "Be not deceived; God is not mocked: for whatsoever a man soweth, that shall he also reap" (KJV). This is what the word of God says and the best response is for us to be honest with him. God wants to deal with issues in more unique ways just as the problems themselves are unique. The principal key is honesty in all our dependency on God. Do you depend on God? Then be honest with him.

God's Word is the truth and that Word has to be in us. The mission motivated life is possible when past hurts are healed. Are you really healed from your past hurts? You are really healed when past memories of hurtful experiences do not raise painful feelings within you. This is the reason why forgiveness remains an essential of life in relationships. God is the God of relationships and forgiveness in those relationships has real impact on you as a person.

Living in un-forgiveness is actually living in bondage. When you do not forgive you remain bound to the persons you are against. Despite that the incident happened a long time ago, the attachment to that person remains intact. The best way to deal with the situation is by using forgiveness. Forgiveness is from God and with God's perspective you can forgive anyone.

One day in Capernaum when people heard that Jesus was in town they began to gather at the house where he was staying and the crowd was so big that people could not easily go in and come out of the house. Four people came with a man who was paralyzed carried on a stretcher. When these people could not go through the door because people were crowded around the door, they made an opening in the roof of this house. They went through a lot of trouble, but they were determined to bring their sick friend before Jesus.

Now, when Jesus saw this, he was moved to say some of the most gracious words. Jesus told the man that his sins were forgiven. This man experienced healing after he was forgiven. Forgiveness is from God to us through Jesus Christ and it is a gateway to the miracles we need in life. The forgiveness of God is backed up by his power. Jesus proved it by performing the miracle of healing on that paralyzed man.

Forgiveness has to be backed up with action. When you are hurting because someone hurt you in the past, your behavior toward that person is usually affected. The most likely reaction is that you would begin to be defensive or aggressive toward such a person. This is the normal human reaction, but when you have been forgiven, your response toward that person becomes favorable. However, when you are forgiven by God, people will always wonder at your responses because of the change that has happened inside you. When you are walking in forgiveness you will respond favorably to people and events instead of reacting to them. When you have been forgiven by God just like that paralyzed man who was forgiven after being lowered through the opening in the roof, you can easily forgive anyone. Finding this kind of forgiveness in Christ is like finding a treasure that makes you forget about everything else unpleasant in your past. It is something that really changes one's life.

In John chapter five from verses one to seven the Bible talks about the healing of another paralyzed man in Jerusalem. In this case, those with physical limitations and other infirmities gathered around the pool of Bethesda waiting for the moving of the water by an Angel. When Jesus came to the pool he saw one man who had suffered with a physical condition for a long time. Jesus asked this man a simple question about his situation. This question can also help us learn something from life and it is about whether you want to get well. Jesus wanted to know if this man at the pool wanted to be healed. Instead of answering the question the man went on to telling his life story. The answer instead should have been, yes sir, I want to be healed.

When this man told his life story it revealed that there are people who were doing better than him because of his condition and this bothered him. Although he had physical limitations, this man was smart enough to know when it was the right time to jump into the pool. However, he was not just able and quick enough to jump in. This man could have been bitter against those who were getting healed. The only way to deal with his difficult experience at the pool was to do what Jesus told him to do and that is to just pick up his bed and walk. Jesus will always come through for you at the right time and his time is the right time. Just walk in obedience to his word and be free from the negative past so that you can be effective at what you do to reach people for Jesus.

A mission motivated life is free from the entanglements of the past. Forget the past and press on to that mark of God's high calling. Dwelling on the negative experiences of the past will not help in making strides toward the mark of that high calling you have in Christ. Move on with your life because God wants to give you a future. Break away from the entanglements of the past.

The man at the pool was trapped in the idea that no one really cared about him. Everyone was reaching his goal except him. He explained to Jesus that no man was ready to help him in his condition. Since Jesus was showing him some empathy, this man opened up and began to explain to him about the difficulties in his past. In other words, he was painting a picture of how people around the pool treated him. This man may have thought that the people around that pool were not good to him. However, Jesus changed the situation and he ended up having the opportunity to forget the difficulties of his life at the pool.

These people at the pool were religious people in a religious city which means they had probably seen the disconnection between real life and religious ideology. This is what made the difficulties he was going through more painful because in religious circles charitable behavior is expected, but it is hurtful when it is not rendered. This man kept hoping and trying and in the end he met Jesus who finally healed him completely. Healing came in a way he never expected, but it manifested because he did what Jesus told him to do and that is, to get up and walk.

When you face discouraging circumstances Jesus has the last words and his words are gracious toward you. He does not condemn anyone here on earth. Jesus wants us to be forgiven so that we can be free. What does he delight in? Jesus delights in taking care of people's circumstances when they let him. He saves and that salvation includes deliverance, healing and protection.

Why does Jesus do all this? He does it because he loves people and out of his mercy he will continue doing what he does without any partiality. He does not condemn people. As a matter of fact, he offers the same opportunities for the righteous and the unrighteous.

When people met Jesus Christ, their needs ended up being met and their lives were changed. Those who could not walk began to walk and those who stepped out to take supernatural walks like Peter who walked on water did it by depending on what Christ said. Walking on water is like living a Christian life. It is hard when you are not obedient to what God has commanded you to do. It is impossible to live as a Christian without God because this kind of life is only possible through Jesus Christ.

Now in Christ we can all walk after the Spirit. If you are

asking yourself whether you can truly live a Christian life, please know that it is possible. You cannot do it by yourself because it is Jesus who makes this walk possible. It is Jesus who told the paralyzed man at the pool of Bethesda to get up and walk. He also told Peter to come to him by walking on water. Jesus still makes people to live holy lives and it is possible when you allow him to do it through you as you respond to him in faith.

Chapter 4

The Love of God

God is affectionately drawn toward us. He loves us so much that he had to give us Jesus Christ so that we can be saved from sin. Jesus is that perfect solution to the human condition. He went to the cross of Calvary for our redemption. Right now, he is in heaven preparing mansions in the Father's house and making intercession for us. Now our hope is to overcome as he overcame. Since Jesus helps us to overcome by his Spirit we have to trust him to help us in time of need.

There is a difference between love and trust. Love is basically available for everyone in whatever condition they may be in. Trust on the other hand is something that he entrusts to individuals depending on what is at stake. God has trusted his son Jesus Christ with the work of salvation in this world. What is at stake are men's souls and souls cost the life of Jesus. Since men's souls are at stake the only one who can be trusted with this work is Jesus Christ. He is the faithful one and no one can be as faithful as Jesus. There is no sin in him therefore death could not hold him captive. God has trusted such a man because he is able to finish the work of salvation as planned.

People have little understanding of the true value of a soul. God knows that value and that is why he wanted Jesus Christ to complete this eternal work of salvation. No one can be trusted with this work, but Jesus Christ the Lamb of God. There is no greater response to the human need for salvation than the one that Jesus has taken for all humanity. Whatever you do in Christ should be rooted in what he has done and continues to do for mankind.

Jesus is the only one qualified to save the world. When John on the island of Patmos learnt that Jesus was able to do for mankind that which no one else could do, he was comforted. We need to reach out for any comfort we can find in Jesus. Only Jesus Christ could face the cross for the world. This is due to the fact that he loves people. He laid his life down for all of us and was able to take it back. Jesus died, was buried and raised from the dead for us to have eternal life. No one could do that because all men have sinned and none could have been able to resurrect from the dead for human race because of sin that is in every man. Only Jesus could face death knowing he could come back from the deep dungeons of darkness and because of his love for us he faced death and conquered it for all of us.

He was not afraid of death because he loves us. If he was hired then he could have abandoned the task. He would have gotten away from anything that could have threatened his life, but since he is the great shepherd he stayed on task. Jesus faced death fearlessly because he loved us and had to overcome death for us all. Jesus loves us all.

God is love therefore Jesus must be love. In the Gospel of John 1:1 the Bible refers to Jesus as being "The Word". The Bible says that in the beginning was the Word and the Word was with God and that Word was God. The Word was God, the same God who is love. Later the Word became a man and that Word is Jesus Christ. Now, here we see God trusting God because of what is at stake, meaning he trusts himself and that surely we all have to trust and believe that God does an excellent work. God depends on himself and he will work through people when they let him.

Jesus did the work of God with a great sense of altruism. Altruism means doing something for someone else without the motive of wanting to be paid for it. Our lives today are impacted by the market economy because of the monetary value tied to what we do. This is basically what molds the way we think and do things in our society.

The true sense of altruism does not encourage you to neglecting yourself. You are an important part in the process of extending that affection to other people. The transaction between God and you involves the aspect of your true self. You have to love yourself first before you can love another person. No one can give what he or she does not have. This is true with love. It is not possible to claim you love your neighbor when you do not love yourself. First take care of yourself to be able to take care of another person. You cannot give what you do not have. This same principle is applicable in our service to God for the people in the world. This is a major key to a mission motivated life.

Today when you give openly, other people can easily misunderstand your giving and may even come up with their own ideas about your motives. Giving is more rewarding when it is done in private because it is done with the idea that God rewards what he sees in private. God's rewards are diverse, generous and perfect and the God who sees in secret has the ability to reward everyone's good works openly.

People can go ahead and make up their own ideas about motives when giving. The disciples who walked with Jesus were not immune to that because they also had ideas and expectations of their own. There is one incident in which the disciple wondered about Jesus and this happened at the well when he was talking to a Samaritan woman. Jesus had put himself in a position like that of the Samaritan woman. He had no means of drawing the natural water just like the Samaritan woman had no means of drawing living water from the spiritual well that Jesus talked to her about. The dividing line had to be crossed and that day the Samaritan woman found the living water she was really looking for in her life.

The disciple's way of thinking was also conditioned just like the Samaritan women. They could not understand why Jesus was talking to a woman at the well. When the disciples were dealing with the "gender" boundary issues, the Samaritan was dealing with the "racial" boundary issues. Meanwhile, Jesus was doing the work of God by breaking the walls of partition. Boundaries were being crossed so that real change in life could be realized.

The Samaritan woman was conditioned in her way of thinking because of the way things were customary done then. Jesus was telling her that the times had now changed. He was really telling her that in him there would be one holy nation with a royal priesthood that would worship the Father in Spirit and truth. On the other hand he was telling the disciples to open up to a new way of ministry. The wall of separation that creates the idea of "them and us" is not something that can help in the mission to the human heart.

We all have to deal with issues that may limit our transaction with God and fellow man, but in Christ these limitations are taken away. God has removed the wall of division between him and us by Jesus Christ. Through Christ our service to God can be done with a sense of altruism.

The first step to practicing altruism is to understand that no one is immune to deception. People tend to think of deception as being from false prophets or teachers when actually anyone can deceive his owns elf. Watch out for self-deception and be open to God's way of doing things. Avoid emotional thinking and promote real change to better the human condition. The answer is truly found in Jesus Christ and he can reach anyone in this world.

The foundation for true altruism is love and that love benefits both the receiver and the giver. It is not only the people on the receiving end who benefit from the acts of love. Those who offer love to other people benefit too. God sees in secret and rewards openly and this means that God cannot forget to reward those who love other people. Their labor of love is not in vain.

We all need to figure out what we want out of this life. Do we want to settle for temporary or eternal benefits? Well, eternal benefits matter and they are not like pleasures that last for a short season. Jesus Christ was able to see people's motives as they later sought him for food after he fed them with bread and fish in one of his meetings. When people sought for Jesus after they were fed by his miraculous provision he cautioned them not only to seek after temporary provisions like food. This is the reason why we must always ask ourselves why we do what we do so as to make sure we are following Christ for the right reasons.

Moses understood this very well when he faced a similar situation in Pharaohs Palace. He had all the pleasures of life at his disposal, but chose not to indulge himself in pleasures that would endure for just a season. What are you looking for in life? Life is full of choices and choosing to follow Christ has its own rewards. Eternal life is a gift that God gives to us and choosing Christ is really choosing eternal life.

A choice like this stems from being able to see beyond what is in the natural. Moses saw him who is invisible and made the best choice of his life. He saw God and seeing God is what we need to do. We need to see him who is invisible. What kind of eyes would see the invisible one? It is eyes like those that Moses had. These were eyes that can see through life enticements and make sense of what God has in his great redemption plan.

It is better to love God than to love the things that he has created. This is what the old life story of Job reveals to us too.

Job was tried on the basis on whether he loved God or not. The accusation against him was that he worshipped God because he was blessed with good things in life. If you love God for who he is then you are on a solid ground. When you love God for what he has given or what he can do for you then you need a true change of heart. You need Jesus Christ to be the foundation of your life. People who overcome when tempted truly love God from the heart. Do you love God enough to obey him? Jesus today still challenges that lack of affection for him. It is easy for us to lose sight of Jesus and just focused on what he can do for us. When we focus on Jesus it means we have all what we really need, eternal life. It is better to obey for obedience to God is the position of power.

In Christ we have the forgiveness of sins and that affords us the opportunity to be partakers of eternal life. That is the position of power. When Adam and Eve sinned in the Garden of Eden it broke God's heart. Due to this fact, man was now going to face all kind of suffering. Man was going to get sick and even experience physical death. This broke God's heart because God loves man and he does not want him to perish. This was the loss of power for mankind.

If man had to take from the tree of life without the chance of being forgiven by God, it could have been more heartbreaking. Imagine man having to go through all the suffering because of sin, but at the same time having to live forever. That would have been horrible. Now we can have life through Jesus Christ for eternity without facing the consequence of sin. Through the blood of Jesus Christ our sins are taken away and now we can have eternal life without the consequences of sin.

God loves you. Do you love him? Do you love him so as to give him everything? To be focused on him so much that everything else takes second place? There may be some things in your life that has taken that first place. The only way to give

God first place is to surrender your life to Jesus Christ.

A long time ago God tested Abraham by asking him to sacrifice the son he loved so much and he obeyed. When he was about to sacrifice Isaac his son, God stopped him and instead provided a ram as a sacrifice. God demands that you give up anything that takes up his place. Only God should become first in your life as he became first in Abraham's life.

You would wonder what was going on in Abraham's mind when God asked him for his son Isaac. Abraham was steadfast, diligent and willing to do what God told him to do. God wanted Isaac and not Ishmael for that sacrifice. God knew exactly what was in Abraham's heart just like he knows what you love and cherish in your heart. It was hard for Abraham to give his son Isaac, but he loved God so much that he just had to obey.

It could probably have been easier for him to give Ishmael than Isaac considering that he had waited for many years to have Isaac. Isaac was that precious to Abraham, but he finally had to obey God. We can all obey just like Abraham obeyed God and end up experiencing God's providence. What happened with Abraham as he sought through his circumstances?

Early the following day he got up as early as he could and did what God told him to do. When Abraham did what God told him to do it signified how much he loved God. When you love someone you will always obey that person. You cannot obey anyone you do not love. This is what God wants from us all. He wants us to love him. What Abraham did shows us what the love for God can do. Since God loves us he will always provide for us. When we are in need he will always be ready to provide for us. He has provided for us through the death and resurrection of Jesus Christ who is God's provision for our redemption.

A lot of what was going on was mainly between God and Abraham because Isaac noticed that things did not really add up. Everything was according to the way things were done when a sacrifice was being offered, but this time the sacrifice was missing. However, God put a word of wisdom in Abraham mouth.

On the way when Abraham was talking to his son Isaac he spoke the Word God revealed. He was saying what God was pointing to the true deliverance from the bondage of sin through Jesus Christ. God was talking about the lamb not just for Israel's deliverance in Egypt, but for all of mankind because the lamb of God Jesus Christ would be made available for the whole world. It is this Word that gives us the opportunity to find freedom from sin. This is the Word that reveals God as the most precious possession. Abraham was talking to Isaac about Jesus Christ the perfect sacrifice for the whole world.

At the altar when Abraham was about to offer Isaac, the provision of God manifested. When Abraham was talking to Isaac about God providing the sacrifice, a ram was already being caught in the thicket. This is the ram that was offered as a sacrifice instead of Isaac. God provided a sacrifice for Abraham just like he has provided Jesus Christ today. Jesus is the Lamb of God. Now it does not have to be Isaac the son of promise or the ram that was caught in the bushes when Abraham was about to offer his son, but the Lamb of God who is Jesus has been provided. Surely God provides for his own people. The Lamb of God is God's provision to mankind and now all of us can come boldly into the presence of God to find mercy in time of need. God's time is the right time and that is why in the fullness of time God sent his son.

Abraham loved God more than he loved his son Isaac. Since Abraham did not withhold his son Isaac, God has not withheld his son Jesus Christ. Just like no one can build God a house for him to live in, only God himself can build that house. No man can give the perfect sacrifice because only God can give the perfect sacrifice and God himself has given us Jesus Christ who takes away the sin of the world.

No matter how much Abraham loved Isaac his love could not exceed the love he had for God. Do you have an Isaac in your life? Is there anything that you might be affectionate to you more than God? Surrender it to God in Jesus name and give God first place. An Isaac in your life could be anything therefore just surrender to God and he will take care of the rest. That Isaac could be your own life. It could also be a habit or a way of thinking that accommodates thoughts that exalt themselves against the knowledge of God. An Isaac could be a selfish pleasure or anything you consider so dear to you above God. Give it to Jesus so that God can take his first place in your life.

Chapter 5

The Will of God

Only Jesus Christ could face the cross for the world. He is the only one who was able to do the will of God so that we can have the opportunity to do his will too. The will of God is what Jesus Christ referred to as the will of the Father. It is an essential part of any believer's life. There is no way any Christian can defeat the forces of evil without doing and being in the will of God. Jesus overcame because he chose to do the will of the Father. You can only overcome evil by doing the will of God as Jesus did.

Please note that it was possible that Jesus could have done his own will when he faced death. Jesus chose to do the will of God the Father. When he communed with the Father on the issue of redemption he tried to see if there were other options. The most dreaded thing he faced was that separation he would go through by dying. Death, depending on what kind it is, separates either man from man or man from God. He found the separation from God to be hard to face.

A man living in sin is separated from God. When God the Father allowed Jesus to bear the sin of the world, he became separated from God. There was no option because the cross was the will of God. In Matthew 26:39 the Bible talks about Jesus and says, "Going a little farther, he fell with his face to the ground and prayed, "My Father, if it is possible, may this cup be taken from me. Yet not as I will, but as you will"(KJV). Jesus did the will of God. He surrendered his will to God the Father and it is through the same will of God where we find

Salvation.

Well, Jesus had his own will and God the Father had his will just like you and I have a will of our own, but Jesus did the will of God instead. The will of God is what really matters. There is a difference between the will of God and the will of man. The will of man gives birth to human nature but the will of God gives birth to Divine nature.

When you are born again, you are born by God's will and you become a partaker of his Divine nature. The seed of God comes into your being. This is possible only by the will of God. The rules of nature have no control over this kind of birth. It only happens when you surrender your will to God. Again, the will of God the Father is what really matters. Are you ready to surrender your will to God? Ask Jesus to come into your heart. Ask him to forgive your sins because sin separates you from God. Anyone who has Jesus has life and has already crossed from death to life as long as he is in Christ.

No one can do the will of God unless he knows what God says. Doing the will of God is a responsibility that stems from knowing what God says. If you do not know what God says, there is no way you can be confident that what you are doing is really the will of God. It is the will of God to sit at the feet of Jesus and acquire the knowledge you need. Every circumstance presents its unique challenge, but knowing what God wants you to do in a particular circumstance is what secures you in doing and being in the will of God.

This means we all have to know what God says to us personally and not just what he says in the written Scripture. What he says to us, right in the situation we face makes the will of God more realistic. This is the reason why we have to present our bodies as living sacrifices to God. There is a price to pay for us to become aware of the will of God. The Scripture in Romans chapter twelve and verses one to two shows us that our being and way of thinking must change for us to know the will of God.

Presenting yourself as a living sacrifice is considered a reasonable service to God, but that goes along with what God wants you to do so that you can sense and do his will in a given situation. Doing the will of God constitutes a closer relationship with God. The communion that goes on with God and man then becomes the means for knowing what God wants us to do.

In Mark 3:35 Jesus says, "For whosoever shall do the will of God, the same is my brother, and my sister, and mother". When Jesus said this he was actually pointing to those disciples who were listening to his teachings. These disciples were engaged in the things of God and since they would definitely be able to know what God wanted them to do as they received insight from the Lord's teachings, they were doing the will of God. You have to walk close to Jesus to really know what he wants to do.

Hearing from God means receiving and carrying out the responsibility of doing what he says. If someone does not do what God tells him to do, such a one is sinning. The good we know we have to do really is revealed from God. It is only possible to do good after that good is revealed to us. This is a big responsibility because if one does not respond according to the good that is revealed, such a one commits sin.

When Jesus faced the cross of Calvary he made sure that what he was doing the will of God the Father. Jesus knew exactly what the Father wanted him to do. Knowing what God wants you to do in any given circumstance is the principal thing in doing the will of God. You can only know his will when your mind is renewed by what you hear or learn from the word of God.

The mission motivated life is only possible when you are set to doing the will of God. Jesus did God's will; we can all do

God's will too. God respects your will. Anyone can do whatever he or she wishes, but has to face the consequences of his choices. Adam blamed Eve only God remained righteous, but Adam and Eve come under the rule of sin. The only way out of sin is by doing the will of God.

Now, when someone says that he has always been a Christian because he or she was born in a Christian family such a one is implying that God does not respect man's free will. The fact is that God does not force people to become Christians by causing them to be born in Christian homes. God did not give man a free will and then later overlook it. Any religion that does not respect man's free will puts people in some kind of bondage. People must be born of God to become Christians and this happens by the surrender of that free will to God. Jesus sets people free when they surrender their will to him and by doing this they are acknowledging that he died for them.

Religious activities are not to be confused for doing the will of God. Jesus warned people not to be fooled by this way of thinking. This is a warning to all of us so that we should not think that being involved in religious activities is really doing the will of God.

Doing the will of God begins at a beginning of a relationship with Jesus Christ. This is the right way to do anything acceptable to God. It signifies that work is not something that is exclusively independent from God.

The work of God should not be about you, but everything about Jesus. It is Jesus doing his work and not you. When this is done through you without the changes of the new birth experience, it means everything you do afterward is just you own work. It means you are still doing you own will. The work of God is really the work of God and not the work of man. That is why when you give your life to Jesus you become one with him and he becomes the one who does the work through you.

What you do would not really be your work, but the work of God.

Those who do the will of God are known by God. Jesus must know you, for you to enter into the kingdom of God. Entering the kingdom of God is only possible through the work of redemption through Jesus Christ. Performing religious work is not a valid way to get into the Kingdom of heaven. It is only valid when you first give your life to Jesus. God must know you. In 1 Corinthians 8:3 the Bible says, "But if any man love God, the same is known of him" (KJV). This is something that stems out of love and not from the performance of wonderful works. What a child of God does should come from the heart that really loves God.

When you love God you will obey him. When you are obeying God it means that you are doing his will. Doing God's will really means God is at work in and through you. We are commanded to love God, not as we love yourself, but with all our heart, soul, mind and strength. Love leads to obedience.

The love we show our neighbor is limited to how much we love our self. The love for God exceeds that love of self. It exceeds that love of self because it demands that God be loved with the whole of our heart, soul, mind and strength. This means the heart does not need to have any reservations for God. It must be willing enough to reflect who God is. God is love therefore you must also love as he loves. He loved the world so much that he had to do something about its condition. Love is courageous enough to cross land and sea just to obtain what it values without having any fear. Love fuels great acts of faith and it helps ordinary people to endure and overcome unimaginable things for the people they love.

Those who have truly loved God have in time past crossed oceans mountains and valleys in search of souls of men. Some have travelled to far places without the hope of returning to their home because they loved God with all their heart. They were doing the will of God because they loved God with all their hearts, soul, mind and strength. Jesus told the disciples that if they love him then they would obey him and by obeying him they really be doing his will. This is what Jesus asked Peter. He asked him three times and Peter even got angry about it. Do you love God?

Love comes with a great responsibility of doing the will of God. When Jesus said this to Peter, he began to talk to him about doing the will of God. He talked to him about the seriousness of doing the will of God. Peter had repented after denying Jesus therefore did not have the guilty conscience, but had doubts about the whole mission he was involved in for three and half years. After seeing what happened during the arrest of Jesus he turned to fishing again. Without Jesus Christ, the hope for the mission was lost.

After the lord's resurrection Peter still decided to gather his friends for a night of fishing at sea. Peter and the rest of the other Apostles earlier said that they had left everything to follow Jesus and the Lord himself commended them for it. At that time the disciples understood that giving up everything else for the sake of the Kingdom was truly rewarding. After the arrest and crucifixion of Jesus the disciples seemed to have lost all hope. They instead decided to go fishing, toiled all night and caught nothing.

Since this was something so serious, Jesus began to talk to Peter about it. Jesus knew they would end up being committed to the mission after receiving the Holy Spirit. After his resurrection Jesus wanted Peter to realize that love is the foundation for doing the will of God. No matter what happened in the past Peter was still capable of doing the will of God. Jesus did not give up on him although he really needed to understand what it meant to follow Christ.

Jesus told Peter that as a young person he was able to go anywhere he desired, but that as an adult he would have to surrender to someone's will and be led into places he would not go into on his own. He wanted Peter to understand what it meant to do the will of God. Jesus was showing Peter what it really meant to do the will of God. He was saying that doing the will of God is something which really stems from a willing heart, full of love for God. When you are an adult you understand what it means to surrender your will to another person. This carries an element of trust and as an adult you can only trust someone after making your own judgment on issues at stake.

When we love God we end up doing his will because we love him. What type of love then should we have for Jesus? Is it like the love we have for our self, our neighbors or fellow believers? Well, we are supposed to love God, our neighbors but we also have to love our fellow believers too? Do we have to love them as we love our self? No, Jesus says that we should love our fellow believers as Jesus himself loves us.

In John 15: 12 Jesus says, "This is my commandment, That ye love one another, as I have loved you (KJV). Jesus taught the disciples to love one another as believers just as he loves them. We should love our neighbors as we love our self and love God with everything within us, but love fellow believers to a point we could lay our lives for them. This means considering what God is doing more important than your own life.

Now, how much does Jesus really love us? Well, the answer is easy. Jesus loves us enough to die for us. In John 15:13 the Bible says, "Greater love hath no man than this, that a man lay down his life for his friends" (KJV). The love that Jesus has for us made him to lay down his life. Man can love his neighbor as he loves himself, but that love is not great enough to cause him to lay down his life for his fellow man. Only the love of God can and it is the same love that motivates us to do the will of God. The love Jesus has for us led him to the cross. He did not avoid death on the cross. Love led him to do God's will. That love will also lead you to do the will of God. Jesus pointed out that it is only love which leads to walking in obedience. If you love Jesus you will obey him.

Love can also cause believers to do things for each other with a great sense of altruism. This in-turn manifests joy in their hearts because they are truly pleasing God. This happens when people walk in love because when they forgive one another from the heart joy wells up from their hearts. Loving God and obeying him is a sign that shows that believers truly love each other.

In 1 John 5:2 the Bible says, "By this we know that we love the children of God, when we love God, and keep his commandments (KJV). Obeying God is the way to love other believers. Obedience to God is doing the will of God and that could even mean sharing a word of encouragement, praying for someone, or just being present for someone in a time of loss. Doing the will of God springs from love and it is a driving force in the mission to the human heart.

Chapter 6

The Gifts to the Church

The most precious gift to the church is the Holy Spirit. The Holy Spirit is the same Holy Spirit that Jesus Christ was anointed with. Jesus went about healing those who were oppressed of the devil because the Holy Spirit was present to heal people. People followed him because of the miracles he did on those who were sick. One thing we have to remember is that God was with him and that is why in John 8: 29 Jesus said, "And he that sent me is with me: the Father hath not left me alone; for I do always those things that please him" (KJV). The Holy Spirit made Jesus to constantly experience the presence of God because was always doing the will of God. This means that no one can do the will of God except by the help of the Holy Spirit. In fact no man really knows how to pray without the help of the Holy Spirit.

The Holy Spirit makes it possible for us to pray according to the will of God. He prays through us according to the will of God. When Jesus Christ was praying in the garden of Gethsemane he wanted to make sure he did the will of God and not his own will. It is different when it comes to the Holy Spirit. The Holy Spirit has no other will, but the will of God. The Holy Spirit is that important that is why King David cried out to God for the Holy Spirit not to be taken away from him.

When God took away the Holy Spirit from King Saul he ended up being tormented by evil spirits and David witnessed what happened to King Saul. David had real fears if the Holy Spirit was to be taken away from him. David could not afford losing the presence of the Holy Spirit in his life.

This is the same Holy Spirit that is in the Church today. The day the Holy Spirit will be taken away from the face of the earth during the rupture, the world will experience destruction and chaos as never seen before. However, it is comforting to know that the Holy Spirit is still here and will continue to work among us until Christ returns. The Holy Spirit is doing wonders among us so that the will of God can be accomplished on earth.

Everyone who comes to Jesus is drawn by the Holy Spirit. This is the reason why through Jesus we now know God by means of his presence as Emmanuel meaning that God is with us. The presence of the Holy Spirit is a fact. Jesus Christ is in our hearts by faith, but the presence of the Holy Spirit is real. The Holy Spirit is the greatest gift that Jesus Christ has ever given to the church. This gift is for everyone who calls upon the name of the lord.

Now, in Ephesians 4:7-8 and 11 the Bible talks about Christ giving gifts. It says, "But unto every one of us is given grace according to the measure of the gift of Christ. Wherefore he saith, When he ascended up on high, he led captivity captive, and gave gifts unto men . . . And he gave some, apostles; and some, prophets; and some, evangelists; and some, pastors and teachers" (KJV). This is the five-fold ministry that has men and women with special abilities given as gifts for the growth of the church. The gifts of the fivefold ministry are given to the church so that it can be edified.

We need the fivefold ministry now more than ever because the Church needs to grow to full stature. The office of an Apostle is still functional. The people in the time of Jesus had the same spiritual needs as we have today. All of these offices are necessary for the Church to be built up to the full stature of the fullness of Christ. The body of Christ needs Apostles to help it mature.

The gift such as the office of the Apostle is still valid today not as a title, but as a position of function. Why? This gift begun to manifest after Christ ascended to the Father in heaven and that is the reason why the Bible tells us that Jesus gave gifts when he ascended on high.

The gifts were given to the Church after Christ went to heaven. Now we may ask, what about the prophets in the Old Testament, where they not already functional before Christ ascended to the Father? Yes, they were functioning and that is in relation to Israel and the first coming of Jesus Christ.

However, the prophets are still here in relation to the Church and the second coming of the anointed one. This is the reason why Christ ascended on high and gave gifts to men. After Christ ascended to the Father that is when he manifested some of the gifts that began to touch lives far beyond race or nationality. The church is not just one race, but many races brought together and made into one person through Christ. This is what is called the Church.

When Christ chose the twelve disciples he called them Apostles. He wanted to prepare them so that they could be sent out. In Luke 6:13 the Bible says, "And when it was day, he called unto him his disciples: and of them he chose twelve, whom also he named apostles" (KJV). Jesus chose these twelve because he was going to train and then send them out. This is the reason why he called them Apostles.

During the time Jesus Christ was training the Apostles he made sure they received everything they needed for the missions ahead. Sometimes they had hands on training and it was exciting, but at times it was discouraging because of spiritual obstacles. They were excited when they casting out demons using the authority of his name and they got discouraged when they could not cast out certain kind of demons. They asked questions on issues they were not sure about and he answered their questions.

At the time he called them they were known as Apostles for sure, but they were not yet prepared to function fully in that office as Apostles. Christ was still training them to take up the challenge as being the sent out ones. Jesus wanted to impact their lives first so that they could later be effective when launching out on their own. The whole three and half years that he had with the Apostles was a time of preparation.

When they were being trained by Lord Jesus Christ they were already called Apostles although they still had their own shortcomings. Since they were all Apostles, they probably assumed some of them were more superior. The ranking system was not as clear to them. However, Jesus showed them that in the Kingdom of God things were set up differently. He confronted this kind of strife and that helped them to later become effective when Christ sent them out.

The Apostles were meant to deal with real life issues and that is why the Apostles were supposed to be prepared for the task. This office was not meant to just be used as a title or as a means to status in society. This office was a position in which they had to function for the sake of extending the Kingdom of God. They were there to meet people's spiritual needs.

One day when the Apostles saw someone casting out a demon in the name of Jesus, but did not follow Jesus along with the rest of the Apostles they told him to stop because he did not follow Jesus like the rest of them. Jesus corrected them and they learnt something new. This was a sure sign that they were to learn a lot about this mission.

When Jesus was on earth the Apostles were still learning a lot about his mission. Please note that when the People in Samaria were not paying attention to the Lord's ministry on their to Jerusalem, the Apostles were willing and ready to call fire from heaven to consume the people just like Elijah did to the fifty soldiers that Ahaziah the King sent to him. In the book of second Kings Chapter one, we are told that Elijah called fire from heaven that consumes the army. Surprisingly enough the Apostles wanted to do the same thing Elijah did to the captain of fifty. They wanted to call fire that would consume the Samaritans who were ignoring their ministry efforts. Jesus had to rebuke the disciples because they needed to know that people are valuable.

People need God's protection because he loves them. This is the reason why Jesus came to seek and save us. The Apostles were reacting in this manner because they were still in training. They were ordinary people with certain misconceptions just like all of us, but Jesus was going to make them capable of accomplishing the mission. Jesus was making them. Jesus will always make you to be ready for the Lord's mission to the human heart.

On another occasion when the disciples came back with lunch for Jesus, he was still talking to a Samaritan woman who came to fetch water at the well. What they had in mind is that Jesus had no reason to talk to women. Probably this was due to the way things were culturally set up. They could not comprehend how a holy man like Jesus would be talking to a woman. Jesus was again taking them to a new level of understanding because he later wanted them to be able to deal with misconceptions and be effective at their mission.

When time came for them to be sent out own their own, they finally did well. This was like field practice or internship for the Apostles. In the Gospel of Luke when Jesus sent the seventy disciples which included the twelve Apostles, they came back rejoicing because of the extraordinary experiences they had. They were excited about it, but that was just a taste of what was to come.

As long as the Apostles were physically with Jesus, they were still not ready to go out on their own. Since he was still with the Apostles in the world he was still their present guide. They had to witness his death and resurrection to make sure they had no doubts about his claims.

Jesus met with most of the disciples and not just the Apostles after he rose from the dead. During one of the meetings he breathed on them and told them that he was sending them as the Father had sent him too. When he breathed on them he told them to wait in Jerusalem until they had received the Holy Spirit. Later when the Apostles received the Holy Spirit they were endured with power from on high and preached the word of God with authority.

Jesus preached the Word of God with authority and people followed him because they saw the miracles that he performed on those who were sick. A lot of people followed Jesus because of the healings miracles he was performing. They saw the miracle he did and that is why they got interested in him.

The disciples also continued to see miracles after they received power from on high as Jesus promised. This happened after he ascended on high that is why he earlier on had to breathe on them before they could receive the Holy Spirit. When he met with the disciples before he ascended to the Father he told them that he was sending them out just like the Father had sent him. During that very moment when he appeared to the disciples behind those closed doors, he breathed on them and commissioned them. In the Church today the Apostles are still the sent out ones and they are here to prepare the believers in the Church for the work of the ministry. The Lord Jesus Christ prepared the disciples for service and now every believer has to be prepared for the task of reaching the human heart.

Peter one of the twelve Apostles experienced a ministry of miracles after Christ ascended to the Father. Despite having denied the Lord when he was arrested, Peter instead became bold after he received the Holy Spirit. Peter had changed into another man. He was not afraid any more. When Peter preached on the same day when he received the Holy Spirit, three thousand people got saved. Later when he was going to a prayer meeting at the Temple, he commanded a disabled man who was seated at the Gate called Beautiful to get up and walk. The man got up and began to walk. He was the same Peter who denied the Lord Jesus the night he was arrested, but the Holy Spirit had changed him in to another man. This change happened from within him. God changes hearts that are as hard as stone into hearts that are obedient. An obedient heart will always do extraordinary things because God will work with such a heart.

Peter also went on to reaching out to the Gentiles. This was a little difficult for Peter since he was a Jew, but he still had to function as an Apostle. He had a new perspective since he had to reach out to the gentiles. He learnt something new as a Jew at the well when Jesus was talking to the Samaritan woman after returning from buying lunch. He must have learnt something after trying to call fire on those disrespectful Samaritan who were unreceptive to their ministry. During all this time Jesus corrected their way of looking at things and helped them to be effective at carrying out their God given mission.

On another occasion when Peter was hungry he saw a vision. God showed him a sheet of four corners that was full of all kinds of animals coming down from heaven. As a Jew it was hard to catch any of those animals for a meal because some of them were considered unclean. After he responded saying that he could not eat any of the unclear animals, God told him not to call anything clean unclean. All this did not make any sense until he was on his way to Cornelius' house. Cornelius was a gentile and when Peter met the people who gathered at Cornelius' house he began to talk to them about his new perception. During the time Peter presented the gospel to the gentiles at this house God had made sure he was prepared for the ministry to the gentiles. Peter finally knew for sure that the gentiles were accepted by God too. He realized that not only certain animals or groups of people were unclean. Every person is unclean without Christ that is why we all needs to be washed in the blood of Jesus Christ our Savior.

It is God who justifies and when he calls anything clean, no man is allowed to call it unclean. Peter finally understood that God did not place Jews above the gentiles. In God's sight men are not just created equal. In his sight they are unclean until they find cleansing from sin through the blood of Christ. God has this power to make those who are not his people to become his people. Among the gentiles Peter was now a changed person despite having had his own misconceptions. Since he was one of the sent out ones, he continued to learn new lessons so as to accomplish his mission. A traditional way of doing things was not going to help him to get through to the gentiles. It took a new perceptive for Peter to reach out to the gentiles that is why we all really need to have the Lord's perspective to reach out to the human heart.

Prophets are also part of what Christ has given to the church. There is a prophetic anointing in the body of Christ today because of the presence of the Holy Spirit. This gift helps the body of Christ to provide spiritual forecast on the end time plan of God. How can this be when Christ in Matthew 11:13 says, "For all the prophets and the law prophesied until John" (KJV). Do prophets still prophesy today? Yes, they do prophecy because the church needs to know God's plan for the Church. There is a need for spiritual forecasting so that the church can know what to do before the return of Christ.

One unique change of life recorded in the Bible is that of Saul who later became known as Paul. He became an Apostle to the Gentiles and was very instrumental in the writing a large part of the New Testament. He was not one of the twelve that Jesus groomed before he went back to the Father. Paul did not have to be there when Jesus walked with the other Apostles for him to later qualify as an Apostle.

Paul was a witness for Jesus Christ and he functioned as an Apostle just like the rest of the other Apostles. At one time he had to testify of Christ in Jerusalem therefore he was determined to go there when he was in Caesarea. In the process of time a prophet came and warned Paul that he was going to face problems if he went into Jerusalem. In Acts 21:10-11 the Bible says, "And as we tarried there many days, there came down from Judea a certain prophet, named Agabus. And when he was come unto us, he took Paul's girdle, and bound his own hands and feet, and said, Thus saith the Holy Ghost, So shall the Jews at Jerusalem bind the man that owneth this girdle, and shall deliver him into the hands of the Gentiles"(KJV). This prophet came from Judea and that happened when Christ had already ascended to the Father. Prophets are still functioning in the Church today.

Remember Jesus Christ said that all the prophets and the law prophesied until John the Baptist. If the prophets prophesied until John the Baptist, how is it that Agabus a prophet from Judea was prophesying so as to warn Paul about what would happen to him in Jerusalem? Well, it is because the prophets before John the Baptist prophesied about the first coming of the Christ therefore the people were supposed to prepare for that coming. People were supposed to prepare for the coming of Christ and they did this by turning away from sin. That is why John the Baptist baptized people in the river Jordan. They had to be ready for the coming of Jesus Christ.

However, we still have to prepare for his second coming and we also need prophets. This is the reason why when he ascended on high he gave gifts to men and they are what we now call the fivefold ministry. They are the fivefold because they consist of offices of the Apostles, Prophets, Evangelists, Pastors and Teachers. Evangelists are a part of the fivefold ministry and are meant to help carry on the mission. When Paul was in Caesarea at the time he received the word of prophecy from Agabus the Prophet from Judea, but an Evangelist by the name of Phillip also met him. When the Apostles earlier on chose men to help wait on tables to alleviate the burden of ministry on the Apostles, Philip was one of the seven who were chosen. This happened at the time when the Grecians and the Hebrews murmured against each other because the Grecian widows were being neglected in the daily services.

These were chosen to wait tables, but Philip was among the seven men of honest report, full of wisdom and the Holy Spirit. However, Philip became part of the fivefold ministry. He was an Evangelist whose preaching was confirmed with signs and wonders. In the book of Acts 8:5-6 the Bible says, "Then Philip went down to the city of Samaria, and preached Christ unto them. And the people with one accord gave heed unto those things which Philip spake, hearing and seeing the miracles which he did" (KJV). Evangelists travel to different places for the purpose of building the Church by calling people to Christ and Philip did it.

Pastors are also part of the fivefold ministry. They are shepherds of the sheep in specific geographical areas of service. Pastors will always take care of the spiritual needs of people in the local area or church. The pastor is not a title, but a position of function in the Church just like the rest of the other offices. Pastors are from God that is why in Jeremiah 3:15 the Bible says, "And I will give you pastors according to mine heart, which shall feed you with knowledge and understanding" (KJV). They feed the Church with knowledge from above and that helps believers to grow in the things of God.

Now, if they do give knowledge about life then Jesus surely could not have left us without Pastors. Jesus knows what is best for us. This is what may have led the Prophet Jeremiah to prophesy about Pastors. They see things that other people cannot see and have the love and patience to take care of lambs and sheep. They take risks by slaying lions and bears like what David the son of Jesse did when his father's flock was attacked by a lion and a bear.

This office is exemplified by Christ who said that he was the great shepherd who gives his life for his people and not run away when there is a threat, a situation scary to any hired shepherd. Pastors are shepherds who are directly involved with the flock and they protect the sheep from anything dangerous. Jesus as an example of a Pastor did not fear to die for us. He died for us and rose from the dead for our justification. He dealt a death blow to the dangers and traps of hell through his death. At the moment anyone who calls on him can be saved.

Teachers are also part of the fivefold ministry. They explain the things of God in ways that make them so clear. In Acts 13:1 the Bible mentions teachers and says, "Now there were in the church that was at Antioch certain prophets and teachers . . ." (KJV). In this Scripture we can clearly see that the Church today needs to have prophets as well as teachers. The purpose of having these gifts in the Church is to help build the body of believers in Jesus Christ so that they can be effective at carrying out the Lord's mission.

Chapter 7

The Holy Spirit

Every believer needs the Holy Spirit to be equipped for God's mission. Now, who is the Holy Spirit? The Holy Spirit is the Spirit of God. Long before the Holy Spirit moved upon the face of the water he had the plan of salvation only made possible through Jesus Christ. He is the third person of the trinity. The trinity has three persons who make up the one and only God. The persons are the Father, Son and the Holy Spirit. The Holy Spirit always does the will of God.

During creation, whatever was spoken into existence came into existence because the Holy Spirit was at work. The Spirit of God manifested what God commanded to come into being. The Father, Son and the Holy Spirit are one and they are always in perfect harmony. This harmony is what is key in what we do together here on earth. The level at which we agree with others determines what can be accomplished. When we walk in agreement with the Holy Spirit we accomplish more than what we can imagine.

This is the same Holy Spirit who was promised to be poured on all flesh. God is a generous God and this is evidenced by what he has done in giving his only begotten Son and pouring out his Spirit on us. What people may claim to possess is not really theirs. God created everything therefore everything belongs to him. The Son and the Spirit of God are precious to him, but he has given to us the precious gift of the Holy Spirit as a seal for our redemption.

Thousands of years ago, God made a promise to pour out his

Spirit on his people. Prophet Joel proclaimed that God was going to pour out his Spirit on all fresh. This means he was going to pour out his Spirit on all people. Many years passed before this promise could be fulfilled, but it finally happened ten days after Jesus ascended to the Father in heaven. This was not just for the disciples because men today are still being filled by the Holy Spirit.

John the Baptist was filled with the Holy Spirit from his mother's womb. This gift is for all people although they all have to personally be able to call upon his name. In the name of the lord there is authority enough to secure salvation from sin for anyone who calls on it. We all have to call on his name before we can receive the gift of the Holy Spirit. You also need to be filled with the Holy Spirit to be effective at reaching the human heart.

In Luke 1: 15 the Bible in reference to John the Baptist says, "For he shall be great in the sight of the Lord, and shall drink neither wine nor strong drink; and he shall be filled with the Holy Ghost, even from his mother's womb" (KJV). However, John the Baptist later said that there was someone coming after him who would baptize people into the Holy Spirit. John the Baptist was baptizing people in water as they were turning away from sin, but Jesus was going to baptize them into the Holy Spirit. Jesus is the one who baptizes into the Holy Spirit and he still does it today.

The fact is that the Holy Spirit will continue to be present with believers forever. Jesus calls the Holy Spirit the comforter. The Holy Spirit comforts, teaches and helps believers to remember the things that Jesus teaches. He talks about Jesus Christ. The Holy Spirit also does many more other things which glorify God. The Holy Spirit guides believers in what is true and reveals what would happen in their future.

The feast of tabernacle revealed an event that symbolized the Holy Spirit as the source of life giving water. In John 7:37-38 the Bible says, "In the last day, that great day of the feast, Jesus stood and cried, saying, If any man thirst, let him come unto me, and drink. He that believeth on me, as the scripture hath said, out of his belly shall flow rivers of living water" (KJV). At the time Jesus spoke these words the Holy Spirit was not given because Jesus was not yet glorified, but when the Holy Spirit was given the disciples became effective in their God given mission.

When Jesus arose he met with the disciples who confirmed that he was truly alive. He actually appeared to the disciples on different occasions for forty days before he ascended to the Father in heaven. On one occasion when Jesus met with the disciples he told them that he was sending them the promise of the Father which is the Holy Spirit. He wanted to make sure that they understood that he was sending them someone who would help them become effective at the task of reaching the human heart.

Jesus wanted the disciples to be equipped for the spiritual task that was ahead. The disciples had to be equipped for the mission. We are also supposed to be equipped for the same mission. They needed to be equipped the same way Jesus Christ was equipped when the Father sent him. We are supposed to be equipped the same way that is why Jesus said to the disciples that they should wait for the promise of the Father.

Now before Jesus ascended to the Father he reminded the disciples to wait for the promise of the Holy Spirit. After spending some time with the disciples for forty days, Jesus finally ascended to the Father. Ten days after he ascended to the Father, the Holy Spirit was poured out on the one hundred and twenty disciples who were waiting for the promise in the Upper Room. When this happened the disciples were changed from the inside. Now, when the disciples received the promise of the Father, the miracle working power was evident in their ministry. Thousands of people got saved on that day of Pentecost alone after Peter preached about Jesus Christ.

A few days later Peter and John were going to pray in the Temple according to Acts chapter three. When they noticed that they had no money to give as arms to the disabled man who sat at Gate called Beautiful, they instead commanded him to get up and walk. After pulling him by the hand his legs gained strength and he began to walk. These disciples were now witnesses for Jesus because the Holy Spirit was with them. In Mark 16: 20 the Bible declares, "And they went forth, and preached everywhere, the Lord working with them, and confirming the word with signs following. Amen" (KJV). The disciples now had power to convince the world that Jesus was the Son of God. They proved it to the people that Jesus was alive and well.

The Holy Spirit gives power to work miracles and has gifts that he manifests to build up his Church. In 1 Corinthians 12: 4 the Bible says, "Now there are diversities of gifts, but the same Spirit" (KJV). This means that the Holy Spirit manifests different gifts. These gifts do not belong to a human being. These are manifestations of the same Spirit of God to help build the church. When believers gather together the Holy Spirit manifests these gifts and those with spiritual needs receive the help they need. If someone needs healing, the Holy Spirit manifests the gift of healing. When someone needs salvation then the Holy Spirit would lead such a one to Jesus Christ. No one can come to God without the help of the Holy Spirit.

The Holy Spirit manifests different gifts in the Church so that the believers can grow. There are gifts that are meant to build the individual believers and there are those meant to build the church. When a believer speaks in an unknown tongue, he builds himself. When someone prophesies, he builds the church. The gifts are distributed as the Holy Spirit wills and it is for the purpose of building the body of Christ.

Speaking in tongues is a gift of the Holy Spirit, but what is it for? In 1 Corinthians 14:2 the Bible says, "For he that speaketh in an unknown tongue speaketh not unto men, but unto God: for no man understandeth him; howbeit in the spirit he speaketh mysteries" (KJV). The purpose of speaking in tongues is to build oneself in the faith. Jude 1:20 says, "But ye, beloved, building up yourselves on your most holy faith, praying in the Holy Ghost" (KJV). This Scripture does not specifically say speaking in tongues, but it says praying in the Holy Ghost which could really mean praying according to the will of God by the help of the Holy Spirit. This kind of prayer aims at building a believer in his most holy faith. Preaching the Word of God on the other hand builds up the Church.

When someone prays in tongues the words he speaks are given to him by the Holy Spirit. These words are a mystery to the speaker, but they are according to the will of God. Anyone listening to someone speaking in tongues cannot understand what is spoken to God in prayer. The speaker then has to trust the Holy Spirit is speaking the right words to God. Human language is not sufficient enough to express everything we need to God. The Holy Spirit is the only one who is capable of speaking to God words that express exactly what he wants. He prays according to the will of God.

We have to be careful not to grieve or quench the Holy Spirit. The Holy Spirit can easily be made grieved or quenched. 1 Thessalonians 5:19 the Bible says, "Quench not the Spirit" (KJV). In Ephesians 4: 30 the Bible also says, "And grieve not the Holy Spirit of God" (KJV). Stopping the Holy Spirit from expressing himself is quenching him. The Holy Spirit always delights in expressing himself to God in ways that please God because he has to guide us. If a believer wants to reach out to another with the love of God, such a one has to yield to the promptings of the Holy Spirit.

Now, when someone sins against God such a one is grieving the Holy Spirit. The Holy Spirit is not happy when there is sin. This is the reason why the blood of Jesus was shed. It was shed so that the Holy Spirit can happily dwell among who were separated from him because of sin. This is the same Holy Spirit every believer is sealed with until the day of redemption. A believer must truly have a close relationship with the Holy Spirit.

How does one receive the gift of the Holy Spirit? In Acts 2:38 the Bible says, "Then Peter said unto them, Repent, and be baptized every one of you in the name of Jesus Christ for the remission of sins, and ye shall receive the gift of the Holy Ghost." (KJV). The first thing one should do to receive the Holy Spirit is to repent from sin. The second thing is to ask God for the gift of the Holy Spirit. When the hundred and twenty disciples received the Holy Spirit on the day of Pentecost, they patiently waited for him until he came upon them.

When the disciples were baptized in the Holy Spirit they receive power from on high so as to accomplish their God given mission. They received the gift of speaking in tongues as well because the Holy Spirit gave them words to speak. The Holy Spirit still does the same thing today. When a believer is filled with the Holy Spirit such a one can speak in tongues, prophesy or speak the word of God without fear. The baptism into the Holy Spirit implies that the person gets completely immersed into the Holy Spirit. The Holy Spirit takes control, the person becomes changed and the power gifts manifest.

However, we have to understand that speaking in tongues in not a sign that someone is baptized with the Holy Spirit. The sign of the baptism into the Holy Spirit is more than just speaking in tongues. Sign and wonders and workings of miracles must follow the one baptized into the Holy Spirit. Speaking in tongues is one of the gifts of the Holy Spirit.

Chapter 8

True Identity

God created man in his own image and that image is in his spirit. Every person has a body, soul and spirit. God is a Spirit and that means man's true identity is in his spirit. In Hebrews 1:5 the Bible says, "For unto which of the angels said he at any time, Thou art my Son, this day have I begotten thee? And again, I will be to him a Father, and he shall be to me a Son" (KJV). God never said this to any of the Angels, but he has said it to his Son, Jesus Christ. Jesus is the Son of God. However, he is not just the son of God; he is also a high priest. Jesus is truly the Son of God as well as a High Priest. This mean he can speak to God on our behalf and then bring us into communion with him. He has made a way for us to have a relationship with God. Without Jesus there is not reconciliation.

Now that Jesus has paid the price for our sins, the way has been made for us to come into God's presence boldly. Jesus is the one who stands in the gap between God and man. He removes that wall of partition that separates man from God. This is the way he has provided the gift of eternal life. We may say that the gift is free when it is not really free. Jesus Christ had to pay for it by shedding his blood so that our sins can be forgiven. It is only Jesus who is qualified to give this gift of eternal life because of what he did to reconcile us all back to God. As the son of God he had to pay the price and as a high priest he let his blood speak a better word to God on our behalf. He will always speak for us to God for eternity.

The time Jesus began his ministry Satan tempted him in

regard to him being the Son of God. Most likely Satan wanted him to doubt who he was. Jesus overcame temptation because he knew who he was. He knew he was the Son of God and as a Son of God he used the power of God in a responsible way. If he had not known who he was and what his responsibilities were, he would not have overcome Satan's temptation.

What is interesting is that years later during ministry time when a legion of demons saw Jesus, they seemed to recognize him as the Son of the most high. How is it that now they could recognize him as the Son of the most high God? Well, it is because during temptation Satan wanted to make sure Jesus doubted who he was. The Serpent did the same thing with Eve when she was tempted to eat from the tree of the knowledge good and evil. Satan was questioning and making suggestions about what God said about that tree. When Jesus was tempted Satan seemed to question his identity. On top of that the tempter also made suggestions that were not consistent with what God wanted. Any time you have questions that bring up doubts about who you are, overcome him the way Jesus did by quoting the written word of God.

Jesus dealt with the question of identity very seriously because it is part of the foundation of his mission to the world. See what the Bible says in Matthew 16:13 and 15 when Jesus and the disciples came to the coast of Caesarea Philippi. The Bible says, "When Jesus came into the coasts of Caesarea Philippi, he asked his disciples, saying, Whom do men say that I the Son of man am . . . whom say ye that I am?"(KJV). These questions are keys to a mission motivated life. Knowing Jesus Christ is by revelation. This knowledge should have that strong personal meaning for you to be established in Christ.

Who you are, is a vehicle to a lot of what you can accomplish in life. This is the reason why you have to make sure you know who you are. You are not the creation of your mind. In other words, you are not what you think you are. What you may think of yourself as being you, will never correctly define who you are.

The truth about you is only defined by what the word of God says. The word of God is the truth. What it says about people is true. What it says about you is also true. Now, what you think about yourself might not be what the word of God says. The way to really know who you are is to let the Spirit of God bear witness with your spirit. Your identity is basically founded in your relationship with God.

As a child of God, the Spirit of God dwells within you. The seed of God is in you and when you become aware of the life within you it then changes your perception. Your name is not your true identity because you can change it at any time, but you cannot change your spirit which is knit to your soul and body. When you become still before God you can enter a realm that makes self-observation possible. In this place you become aware of internal activities in your own being and they point out to who you really are. The part of you that is aware of these activities is you. That is your "spirit man" or the inner man.

Watching oneself from within can have significant effect on how one's own life. When you know for sure that God is really watching you that is when real change begins. That is why the word of God is likened to a mirror that helps us to make the changes in life for better. In this same experience you become one with God by the same Spirit. If you are not one with God, it means you are still separated from him because of sin. Jesus is the one who shed the blood that cleanses us from sin.

Through Jesus we change from the person we call the "old man" to what we call the "new man". Through Jesus Christ our identity changes to that of a child of God.

Paul the Apostle said that it was no longer him that lived, but Christ lived in him. In Galatians 2: 20 the Bible says, "I am crucified with Christ: nevertheless I live; yet not I, but Christ liveth in me: and the life which I now live in the flesh I live by the faith of the Son of God, who loved me, and gave himself for me" (KJV). Paul was saying that Jesus had taken over. When people looked at Paul, they were instead seeing Jesus Christ (the new man) who was manifested from within him. Paul was saying that people should just watch the way he lived and they would know who he is. Paul was a child of God and his identity was rooted in that "father son" relationship with God.

Chapter 9

Spiritual Warfare

The mission motivated life knows how to overcome spiritual forces in the spirit world. We have to understand that man lives in both the natural and spirit world. The conflicts that occur in the spirit world influence the natural world. The spiritual conflict that is happening right now actually started a long time ago and every person in this world is now part of it. You are part of that spiritual conflict, but the good news is that you are positioned to overcome in every spiritual conflict as a child of God.

In Ephesians 6:12 the Bible declares, "For we wrestle not against flesh and blood, but against principalities, against powers, against the rulers of the darkness of this world, against spiritual wickedness in high places" (KJV). This means we fight against spirit beings that are not visible to our natural eyes. These entities or beings are strategically placed and their intention is to destroy you and those you love. They use deception, lies, fear and much more to destroy the souls of men.

Those who believe in Jesus Christ must be aware that they are involved in a huge spiritual conflict and that God has provided a way for overcoming spiritual forces. To overcome these forces God's full armor must be utilized. In verse thirteen of the same chapter the Bible tells us to put on the whole armor of God which protects us from the attacks of the enemy. When you encounters the evil day at some point in life the full armor of God is able to protect you as a child of God. This is God's complete protection for you as a child of God and you need to wear it at all times.

Where did this war start? Well, this war started in heaven. In the book of Revelation 12:7-8 the Bible declares," And there was war in heaven: Michael and his angels fought against the dragon; and the dragon fought and his angels, And prevailed not; neither was their place found any more in heaven" (KJV). In heaven the forces of evil were defeated. In verse nine of Revelation 12:9 the Bible says, "And the great dragon was cast out, that old serpent, called the Devil, and Satan, which deceiveth the whole world: he was cast out into the earth, and his angels were cast out with him" (KJV). Those who belong to Jesus are engaged in a spiritual war. When they remain in Christ their victory is guaranteed.

Jesus has defeated the Devil here on earth. This is the same Devil who was defeated in heaven. When Jesus was tempted by the Devil he overcame. When he was crucified he died, but rose again from the dead. This was a hundred percent victory. Actually this was not his first victory against Satan. Jesus himself said that he saw Satan fall from heaven like lightning. When there was war in heaven Satan was cast out of heaven and he got out of there as fast as he could. On earth also Jesus defeated Satan for us through the cross of Calvary. We can now personally be part of what Christ has done through that cross. Now all believers have the legitimate authority over the forces of evil through Jesus Christ. In that name of Jesus believers have spiritual authority.

The spiritual authority of every believer lies in the fact that he is a child of God. Who you are matters. In Acts 19:13-15 the Scripture says, "Then certain of the vagabond Jews, exorcists, took upon them to call over them which had evil spirits the name of the Lord Jesus, saying, we adjure you by Jesus whom Paul preacheth. And there were seven sons of one Sceva, a Jew, and chief of the priests, which did so. And the evil spirit answered and said, Jesus I know, and Paul I know; but who are ye?" (KJV). This is an important question. Who are you? Who you are, has a lot to do with who you are related to and not on what you can do. Who you are on the other hand has a lot to do with what you can do. It is not really what you think you can do, but what you can really do because of who you are. You have to back up your claim. When Jesus claimed he could forgive sins he proved it by healing the paralyzed man who was brought before him. It was possible for him to heal because he is the Son of God. This is what the seven sons of Sceva most likely misunderstood.

We have to understand that the identity of the seven sons of Sceva was limited to that of an earthly status. Strength in numbers did not help them despite having a father with religious authority as the chief of the priests. Status and strength in numbers meant nothing to the demonic forces that they confronted. They were seven of them, but still remained powerless. Power travels in relationships; when you become a child of God you get positioned for spiritual strength because you are related to God.

When serving God religious titles can easily cause power to dissipate because it inflates that self-made self. The Bible encourages us to die to that self. When a child of God learns how to avoid being puffed up, it can lead to being effective against the forces of evil. It is not what you think you are, but who you really are as being a child of God that matters. Paul the Apostle was wise enough to see through the deception of social status and as a result he ended up pursuing the power of God in ways that pleased God. In other words, he humbled himself and made sure he knew who he was and that is why he was able to continue casting out demons, raising the dead and preaching the gospel of Jesus Christ to the unreached.

The power of God rested on Paul and as an Apostle that is why he was motivated to fulfill his God given mission. He was chosen by God for the purpose of edifying the body of Christ and he did it well. At the end of his life he even mentioned that he had fought a good fight. He walked in humility so as to let the power of God rest upon him. He is truly a good example for us from the book of Acts.

If you are a child of God, it means you have a "father son" relationship with God. This father son relationship is not something that the mind makes up. It is something that really happens when one surrenders his or her will to God through Jesus Christ. Actually the nature of God becomes part of anyone who surrenders himself to God. This surrender of self to God starts with the act of the will and ends up in the change of heart and that is only made possible through Jesus Christ. The Spirit of God comes into anyone who surrenders to God and that same Spirit who comes in cries to God saying "Abba Father" because it is the Spirit of sonship. This is important in regard to what Christ has done and still continues to do on earth by his Spirit. When this relationship is established, the individual who becomes a child of God is able to effectively deal with demonic forces in spiritual warfare.

Now, to rescue people from demonic powers one has to triumph over sin by first becoming a child of God. If you indulge in sin it means you are operating in the domain in which demons have dominion over and in those areas demons have power over human beings. In Christ they do not have power over you because you are freed from sin through the death and resurrection of Jesus Christ. As a child of God demons have no power over you. This power differential has been made possible through the blood of Jesus Christ. As a child of God, your relationship with him affords you the ability to overcome and defeat demonic forces. This ability becomes a reality when your sins have been forgiven. This is what constitutes spiritual authority which is available only through Jesus Christ.

When Christ was tempted after fasting for forty days, Satan brought up the issue of sonship. Satan wanted Christ to prove he was a son of God by using his power as a son of God to turn stones into bread. Three and a half years later, at the time Christ was being crucified people also demanded that he should come down from the cross to prove he was the "Son of God". They did not realize that the cross was really a part of God's plan that is why he did not need to save himself. God's plan was for our redemption and he completed this special work as planned. You can also be part of that plan and that is why now is the time you should be sure you are a child of God.

God is a God of justice and has no partiality. The shedding of the blood of Jesus tells us that he has no favorites. The Angel of death could have killed every firstborn in Egypt, whether Egyptian or Hebrew. God shows no partiality. When the blood of a lamb was used to mark the door posts, it signified that the firstborn in that house was already dead. That is why when the Angel of death came to the door marked with blood he passed over it. In houses marked with the blood of lambs no first born was killed by the Angel of death.

This Angel of death is passing through this land and those without the mark of the blood of Christ at the door of their hearts cannot avoid the Angel of death. The Angel of death passes over us when we have been forgiven by Jesus Christ and his blood has cleansed us from all sin. The blood of Jesus Christ is like the blood of that lamb in each Hebrew household. The markings of the blood of that lamb signify deliverance instead of death. The blood of Jesus speaks a better word to God for us all.

Children of God are marked with the blood of Jesus Christ. This is him a high priest. Jesus intercedes for us. God told Adam that he would end up dying if he ate from the tree of knowledge of good and evil. Now to be saved from death man has to be marked with the blood of Jesus Christ. Man has to be forgiven so that he can be reconciled to God. Are you marked with the blood? Are you really a child of God? A believer can only reach out to other people after he has been reconciled to God. Reconciliation is really what God is doing in this world and to be part of it one has to be reconciled to God. Be reconciled to God.

If you are not sure you are a child of God, take time to ask Jesus Christ to come into your heart. In this personal and private time, talk to God about any sin in your life that come to mind. Confess every one of them to God until you know he has heard you. Tell Jesus that you do not want to live in sin anymore. Ask him to forgive all your sins so that he can be your Savior. Talk to God until you have mentioned everything you think is unpleasant to him in your life and then thank him for accepting you just as you are. Thank him for the way he has made it possible for you to surrender your will to him so that you can become a child of God. At the end say "Amen" meaning that you would like to have everything you have mentioned to be done as you have asked. All this has to be done in the name of Jesus Christ. Legitimate authority from God is what a believer needs in spiritual conflict and as a child of God you have it. Walk in obedience to God's word because that will make you to have that authority against all forces of evil.

In the gospel of John 20:21 the Bible says," Then said Jesus to them again, Peace be unto you: as my Father hath sent me, even so send I you" (KJV). Please understand that it is only those who believe in Jesus Christ who have that legal authority to serve God because they are sent by Jesus Christ. In Mark

16:15 the Scripture also says, "And he said unto them, Go ye into all the world, and preach the gospel to every creature" (KJV). The only way to take up spiritual conflict and come out a victor is by being spiritually connected to Jesus Christ. God has planned for you to succeed in your involvement with him. He wants you to overcome every obstacle in the mission to the human heart. This mission can only be successful through Jesus Christ.

Chapter 10

Confronting Forces of Darkness

The mission to the human heart must be accomplished through the spiritual authority found in the name of Jesus Christ. Believers in Christ have power over demonic forces. Demonic forces are set out to oppose anything that has anything to do with Christ. They aim at killing people in any way they can, but in the name of Jesus Christ they do not stand a chance. The name of Jesus Christ is so powerful that it can be used to expel any demon that has ever existed.

Believers can be successful in reaching out to the human heart by confronting these forces of darkness. Ignoring the fact that demons exist is detrimental to mission to the heart of men. In the mission to reach the human heart beware that there are forces out there waiting to try to stop you. Are you going to let them stop you? No. They could not stop Jesus therefore they should not be allowed to stop you.

Jesus dealt with demonic forces more effectively and he is an example to us on how to defeat them. He taught his disciples to cast out demons in his name and that is why every believer must know how to cast out demons. Jesus taught the disciples to cast out demons and they became good at it.

When Jesus began his earthly ministry he confronted demons in men. At one time when he was teaching at the synagogue in Capernaum he encountered a demon possessed man right in the place of worship. Jesus knew what to do about the situation. He also knew that he had power over all the power of the enemy and since he had power over this demon, he cast it out.

Children of God have authority over demonic forces just like Jesus had authority. As a matter of fact he has delegated this authority to those who believe in him. Do you believe in Jesus Christ? You have power to cast out demons. Jesus cast out demons and set men free from demonic bondage. Casting out demons is part of what we are supposed to do to build the Kingdom of God.

One thing interestingly fascinating about casting out evil spirits is just how real the spirit world becomes. It is an eye opener to the realities of the unseen world. If you have had the opportunity to cast out demons you may have probably been surprised at the way they seemed to have known your name or your life story.

When casting out demons, make sure your life is right with God. Do not attempt to cast out a demon when you knowingly live in sin. Make sure you are prayerful. Prayer makes you to be much closer to God and when you are close to God forces of evil cannot prevail against you. Demonic forces are aware of a lot of things that involve human beings. When Jesus was preaching the gospel of the Kingdom of God he confronted some demons that knew who is.

In Mark 5: 6-7 the Bible says, "But when he saw Jesus afar off, he ran and worshipped him, And cried with a loud voice, and said, What have I to do with thee, Jesus, thou Son of the most high God? I adjure thee by God, that thou torment me not" (KJV). The evil spirits identified Jesus as being the Son of the most high God and knew for sure that they would all be facing judgment any time soon. This is the reason why they asked him not to torment them, but to instead send them into a head of swine. In the presence of Jesus they seemed to comprehend that judgment is coming. They seemed to have some insight about what is going to happen in the future because the same Jesus they ran from in heaven was now on earth.

When you are working in areas where there is a lot demonic activities, the presence of God that you carry into those places exposes their presence. They usually manifest in different ways. In some cases they scream out aloud and when you are conducting a Christian meeting they draw so much attention that can easily be a disturbance to the meeting. You need to know how to discern what is going on in a meeting.

When people are being prayed for in a meeting you have to realize that it is not every fall to the floor that signifies the power of God. When someone screams with eyes rolled backward and fall violently it shows that the person is overtaken by another entity. This means that you have to exercise the authority of the name of Jesus to cast out that entity. In most cases when they come back to their senses they usually do not know what happened to them. This shows that the entity is most likely a demon and the power of God just exposed it. When this happens, cast it out in the name of Jesus.

Some of these spirits are familiar spirits and familiar spirit can fascinate the unsuspecting by the way they reveal other people's life secrets. This can be sometimes mistaken for the "word of knowledge". Get to discern what is behind the manifestation and you will know if God is it. In 1 John 4:1-3 the Bible says, "Beloved, believe not every spirit, but try the spirits whether they are of God: because many false prophets are gone out into the world. Hereby know ye the Spirit of God: Every spirit that confesseth that Jesus Christ is come in the flesh is of God: And every spirit that confesseth not that Jesus Christ is come in the flesh is not of God: and this is that spirit of antichrist, whereof ye have heard that it should come; and even now already is it in the world" (KJV).

What is noticeable when dealing with evil spirits is that they cannot pray through that simple sinner's prayer. There are certain areas of the sinner's prayer they cannot pray through although some people might think the sinner's prayer is just another modern religious tradition. The fact is that demons cannot pray through certain words especially words that talk about the "blood of Jesus" "forgiveness of sins" or "Jesus is raised from the dead" without having to react to them with some resistance. At certain points in the sinner's prayer they may start hissing, screaming and shaking violently. In such cases all you have to do is command them to come out of the person in the name of Jesus. If you live a prayerful life the whole event can only take but a short time.

What is the problem when casting out a demon is taking too much energy and time? When it is taking too long, it means there is a good reason why. When Jesus cast out a demon his disciples could not cast out after he came down from a mountain where he was transfigured he explained to them why they could not cast it out. The disciple waited for the time to find out what really happened since they could not cast out this demon. Did they lose their spiritual power over demonic forces? They probably remembered the time they went out for the very first time and came back rejoicing since demons were all subject to them. They thought maybe something was terribly wrong somewhere. As soon as they got into the house they asked him why they could not cast it out and he told them the reason why they could not.

In Mark 9:28-29 the Scripture says, "And when he was come into the house, his disciples asked him privately, Why could not we cast him out? And he said unto them, This kind can come forth by nothing, but by prayer and fasting" (KJV). Jesus revealed to them that they were dealing with a different kind of a spirit. They were dealing with a kind that requires a certain level of seriousness. You have to be serious enough to take time to pray and fast so as to deal with demonic forces. As long as you have the mission of reaching the human heart there is a need to be serious. When you are serious enough to pray and fast to get over spiritual obstacles then you stand a good chance to reach the human heart.

The other reason it might take long to cast out evil spirits is the fact that there might be an agreement between the possessed and the demon. The possessed person could be benefiting from the demonic activities therefore may not want to be freed. They key here is "agreement". When someone is possessed by a demon, but agrees with the demon because of what he can get out of it, then that connection can cause delays in deliverance.

In Acts 16:16-19 according to Paul the Bible says, "And it came to pass, as we went to prayer, a certain damsel possessed with a spirit of divination met us, which brought her masters much gain by soothsaying: The same followed Paul and us, and cried, saying, These men are the servants of the most high God, which shew unto us the way of salvation. And this did she many days. But Paul, being grieved, turned and said to the spirit, I command thee in the name of Jesus Christ to come out of her. And he came out the same hour. And when her masters saw that the hope of their gains was gone, they caught Paul and Silas, and drew them into the marketplace unto the rulers" (KJV). The demon came out of this young woman because Paul used the name of Jesus Christ.

Now when you use the name of Jesus and the demon continues to resist, the Lord sometimes can reveal that there is a bond of agreement in the case and that insight can help to break that bond. If the possessed can converse with you then ask them to denounce that connection and then cast that demon out in the name of Jesus. Make sure you say, "In the Name of Jesus Christ" and not "In Your Name". In Mark 16:17 the Bible says, "And these signs shall follow them that believe; In my name shall they cast out devils; they shall speak with new tongues"

(KJV). This Scripture refers to his name as being the Name of "Jesus Christ". There is authority in that name.

The Holy Spirit is here on earth for a reason and he is not timid. The Spirit of God is here on earth for serious business. When the church learnt that they could not afford to play religion after the death of Ananias and his wife the church began to be serious. Since their death was brought about by the lie that they both agreed upon the Church changed the way they approached their dealings with God.

God is able to back up his word by his Spirit and demon power knows this is true. In James 2:19 the Bible says, "Thou believest that there is one God; thou doest well: the devils also believe, and tremble" (KJV). As a believer you have the power to defeat any demon, just walk in obedience and God will back up his Word with sign following. Remember that Satan was defeated in heaven when there was war up there and he has also been defeated on earth since the blood of Jesus testifies to this fact. Remember to be strong and courageous because God has given you the kingdom.

Chapter 11

Taking Care of Yourself

It is important for a believer to take care of himself physically, emotionally as well as spiritually. Not paying careful attention to one's well-being can eventually cause problems in one's ability to effectively help people. What is the foundation for self-care? The foundation for self-care is love.

In Matthew 22:37-39 the Bible says, "Jesus said unto him, Thou shalt love the Lord thy God with all thy heart, and with all thy soul, and with all thy mind. This is the first and great commandment. And the second is like unto it, Thou shalt love thy neighbour as thyself" (KJV). When you love yourself you will definitely care for yourself. Caring for other people is not easy to do when you do not care for yourself. It starts with love. You have to love yourself and caring for yourself really stems from that same love you have for yourself.

One of the things to keep in mind is that your effectiveness will always depend how well prepared you are for spiritual activities. Prayer is important in caring for yourself. People who do not pray may not do well when facing temptations. The danger here is that a believer can easily fail when tempted if he is not prayerful. In Matthew 26:40-41 the Bible says, "And he cometh unto the disciples, and findeth them asleep, and saith unto Peter, What, could ye not watch with me one hour? Watch and pray, that ye enter not into temptation: the spirit indeed is willing, but the flesh is weak" (KJV). Prayer prepares a believer for times of temptation. However we also have to remember that it is the will of God for us to pray without stopping. A prayerful person is an overcomer in life.

Somehow people who pray a lot will see things other people consider to be hard experiences as not being hard. This could be due to the fact the prayer prepares them to be ready for life situation. When a believer is in constant communion with God such a one is bound to know the plan God has in a particular issue in the days ahead. The Spirit of God is the Spirit that reveals the future.

Prayer is more than speaking a number of words that end with the word amen. Prayer is meant to change your future. It is meant to change anything that is not in the will of God into what God wants done. You have to be in agreement with God that is why you have to pray in that name of Jesus. When you are in agreement with God it means you are turning things into what you want although it is God really doing it because it is his will that is being done.

A believer needs to have a clear picture of what the will of God is to change the current situation into what he wants through prayer. Jesus gave us an example on how to change things. If you cannot find figs on a fig tree change the future of that fig tree. Is that destructive? No. If what God wants to do is hindered what he does to change things is the most perfect thing to do. If the mountain in front of you is becoming a real obstacle then speak to it. You tell it to move out of your way.

It is easy to forget about taking care of yourself when you are so busy. This is what some people were a concerned when

Jesus got too busy doing ministry. In Mark 3: 20 the Bible says, "And the multitude cometh together again, so that they could not so much as eat bread" (KJV). At this point those who cared much about Jesus just wanted to go and pull him away from what he was doing for a break. The people who knew Jesus cared so much for him.

Sometimes you may just begin by ministering to just one person and before you know it you have a good size gathering that ends up taking a little more of your time. When something like this happens it means the Lord has opened a door to the hearts of people around you. Such a gathering may eventually come to a point where it needs a pastor. This is when things begin to really get busy. This kind of a situation can be demanding, but it is alright to make the needed adjustments so as to continue being effective. The pastor who assumes leadership in such a group must definitely know how to take care of himself first so that he can take care of others.

A pastor who prays knows how to spiritually take care of himself. When he is committed to prayer it could be a sure sign he can prevail in prayer for his people. Pastoral care is about meeting the spiritual needs of the people and having discernment enough to help protect and lead the people in the right direction.

A pastor has to penetrate deep into the spirit world for him to be able to prevail against the enemies of the souls of men. A pastor who does not pray will eventually not be able to spiritually care for his people. A pastor must be a man or woman of prayer because prayer promotes spiritual growth in a congregation.

In Galilee Jesus was taken care of by some women who prepared meals for him and his disciples. These are some of the women who watched him from a distance on the crucifixion day. Jesus had a network of friends and followers who made sure he was attended to well enough. Jesus even had a secret disciple who requested for his body from Pilate after the crucifixion. In John 19:38 the Bible says, "And after this Joseph of Arimathaea, being a disciple of Jesus, but secretly for fear of the Jews, besought Pilate that he might take away the body of Jesus: and Pilate gave him leave. He came therefore, and took the body of Jesus" (KJV). It is important to have a social network of friends who care about you. Jesus had a group of friends therefore it might be something you might need when you are under difficult circumstances. There are times when you may feel emotionally down, but the presence of a friend in such times would cheer you up and make your life easier to handle.

You are also a very important piece in this support system. The mission to the human heart can prove exhausting as long as you have obstacles in your way. Learn to wait upon the Lord. This is the reason why the Bible in Joshua chapter one and verse six says that we should be strong and courageous. No one will ever know what temptation is until he has committed his life to Jesus Christ. People will never know spiritual warfare until there is something great in their future.

The book of Judges has a record of a story of the tribe of Dan. During the time the tribe of Dan was still looking for land to possess, there was a man by the name of Micah who hired a priest for his family. One day a few men came from the tribe of Dan who noticed Micah's priest. The men had noticed that a group of nice behaved people called the Sidonians live in a good land that they wanted to possess. They enquired from Micah's priest if they could attack this group of people and win. The priest told then that it was going to be alright for them to attack that Sidonian group. Although there was another group of Sidonians the two groups had no dealings with each other.

Now, the tribe of Dan realized that this group of nice people had no way of joining with the other Sidonians group therefore they took advantage of that and decided to attack. When the tribe of Dan attacked the Sidonian group that had no dealing with the other Sidonian group in the area they conquered them. If these people were joined to the other group, they could probably been able to defeat the tribe of Dan. What we see in the story recorded in Judges chapter eighteen is something that can help us learn that we all need to network with other people. People who care about you will watch out for you. They will support you when you are in need because they care about you.

When you develop a strong prayer life, it creates a strong support system the world has ever known. As soon as you start facing opposition in unexpected ways in your life you will always have a way out. Your connection with God through Jesus is the strongest and most vital connection for your spiritual survival. It is important for you to survive any spiritual ambush so that you can accomplish the mission God has for you. You can only take care of certain things that you face by prayer. This is what David the son of Jesse did according to what we see recorded in the first book of Samuel.

One day in the life of David the Amalekites made an invasion in Ziklag and on that day David was out of town and the Amalekites took his family captive. When he came back into town he found the city on fire and his people taken captive. This made him to be distressed. He wept for his family and the men he was with also wept for their families until they had no more strength left to continue weeping.

Surprisingly enough the men he was with began planning to stone him to death. These men seemed to have lost their mind. This can make you wonder how the idea of stoning David could have solved this problem. In the midst of that disturbing circumstance David came up with an excellent response. He cheered himself up and then consulted with God. In 1 Samuel 30:6 the Bible says, "And David was greatly distressed; for the people spake of stoning him, because the soul of all the people was grieved, every man for his sons and for his daughters: but David encouraged himself in the Lord his God" (KJV). In this situation David encouraged himself in the Lord.

David did not only encourage himself in the Lord, he also consulted God on this terrible situation. He asked for the Ephod from the priests so as to inquire of the Lord about the situation he was going through. In 1 Samuel 30:8 the Bible declares, "And David enquired at the Lord, saying, Shall I pursue after this troop? shall I overtake them? And he answered him, Pursue: for thou shalt surely overtake them, and without fail recover all"(KJV). Pray to God in whatever circumstance that you are facing. Call unto him and he will answer your call.

David prayed to God. He asked for the Lord's guidance and the Lord guided him. David ended up recovering everything he had lost in the invasion. When you are guided by God you are bound for success. What your enemy has taken from you will eventually be recovered.

When you become a child of God you inherited a lot of good things in his family, but his enemies also become your enemies. God has cut a covenant with you as a child of God and it is made effective through the blood of Jesus Christ because of his death. We receive forgiveness through the blood of Jesus Christ, but also face new enemies. Believers face conflict all the time and that's why Paul the Apostle said that we do not fight against flesh and blood, but against principalities, powers, rulers of the darkness of this present world and against spiritual darkness in the high places. There is a diabolical structure of unseen spirits in the spirit world and as a believer they are your enemies.

When people surprisingly begin to talk against you for no good reason, it is those same evil spirits that are working their way to try to bring you down. People are not your enemy. Satan is your enemy because he is God's enemy. What belong to God belongs to you because you are in a covenant relationship with him. Paul the Apostle encountered such forces during his ministry too. When he was with Silas he cast out a demon from a young woman and ended up being jailed for it. God came through for both of them in prison by causing an earthquake and eventually they were set free after winning the jailer and his family to the Lord. When these things were happening Paul was able to discern what was happening between the spirit and the natural world. This is the reason why Paul was successful at dealing with some of most troubling circumstances. Paul was facing God's enemies, but he knew that he was going to win because these were God's own battles.

In the book of Acts it is recorded that Jesus appeared to Paul commended him for the testimony he gave of him in Jerusalem. At the same time something just opposite was happening in the city. In Acts 23:11 the Bibles says, "And the night following the Lord stood by him, and said, Be of good cheer, Paul: for as thou hast testified of me in Jerusalem, so must thou bear witness also at Rome (KJV). Jesus was saying well done Paul; you did a great job you are now going to Rome. Contrast this to what was happening in the city. Something opposite from what Jesus said to Paul was taking place in the city. Since the battle belongs to the Lord it was won and that is why Paul later ended up in Rome.

In Acts 23:12-13 the Bible also says, "And when it was day, certain of the Jews banded together, and bound themselves under a curse, saying that they would neither eat nor drink till they had killed Paul. And they were more than forty which had made this conspiracy" (KJV). More than forty people had a plan in place against Paul when Jesus had already talked to him about going as far as Rome. It is amazing that some people can seriously plot to harm those who care about others.

However, in this case only the plan that Jesus Christ had of letting Paul go as far Rome prevailed. When you keep the spiritual connection with Jesus circumstances have no power to derail God's plan. God is able to do more than what we can ask or imagine. The plan of man cannot succeed against the plan of God.

Remember that the mission we have in Christ aims at reaching the human heart. When people go overseas as missionaries they aim at reaching the human heart. The "Go" part of the great commission involves a lot of activities, but what really has to be reached is the heart. Every heart has a key that unlocks it and Jesus Christ gives keys to those he sends.

It is time for us to take the keys and use them. Take the keys of the Kingdom now in Jesus name.

About the Author

Rev. M. Mubiana gave his life to Jesus in June 1983 and has ever since been preaching the gospel of Jesus Christ to the nations. He attended a Discipleship Training School (DTS) a school run by Youth With a Mission (YWAM) in 1989 and studied at Kaniki Bible College for two years from 1990 to 1991. Later at YWAM he also completed the School of Church Planting and Leadership (SCPL) for his church planting ministry and a Teachers Training Course which certified him to teach from the Principle Approach perspective at Christian Heritage School in Tyler in Texas.

Rev. Mubiana is an ordained minister of the gospel and has been ordained since November 1996. He has planted churches like River of Life Church now called Glad Tiding Mission in Francistown Botswana, Bimbe Christian Fellowship in Lusaka, and Lively Stones Church in Livingstone which has also continued to plant several sister churches in Zambia Africa. He has also earned his Associate in Arts at Tyler Junior College, a Bachelors and Masters in Social Work at Stephen F. Austin State University.

To contact the author please email: mubiana@live.com

Or Call:

409-761-7467

www.ingramcontent.com/pod-product-compliance
Lightning Source LLC
Chambersburg PA
CBHW071323040426
42444CB00009B/2071